KU-223-915

*your brilliant wedding speech

essentials

helen smith

foulsham 1139765

LONDON • NEW YORK • TORONTO • SYDNEY

foulsham

The Publishing House, Bennetts Close, Cippenham, Slough,
Berkshire, SL1 5AP, England

ISBN 0-572-02762-1

Printed in Great Britain by Cox & Wyman Ltd, Reading, Berks.

Contents

Introduction

So you've been asked to make a wedding speech. Congratulations! This is your chance to tell the world what you know and really think about the bride and bridegroom, in your own words. And remember, thousands of people do it every day, right across the world – and most of them will be first-timers as nervous as you. So don't worry! Speeches should be enjoyable both to listen to *and* give, and this book should help you to achieve both.

This book is suitable for use by both first-time and experienced speech-makers:

- If this is your first time as a speech-maker, and the very thought of speaking to a crowd makes you quake, don't panic. This book will help you to organise your thoughts and find what you need, and even give you some new ideas for a really memorable speech, whatever your role and whatever the circumstances. Read it thoroughly before trying to put a speech together, and then sit down and use what you've learned to make a first attempt. You can then dip into particular chapters for extra help or suggestions when needed.

- If you have previous experience of giving speeches or presentations – whether at work or socially, even at other weddings – some of the initial chapters may sound familiar and you may be able to skim through some sections quite quickly. This book will be of most use to *you* in explaining procedure, giving you new ideas for presentation or content, showing you how to handle particular situations, and helping you to know what to expect from your fellow speech-makers.

What this book contains

The Basics of Wedding Speeches tells you what to expect, who says what and when, and what you mustn't forget to include in your speech. As not all weddings follow this formula, we then look at the expectations at 'informal' weddings, second marriages and those of other faiths and cultures.

Planning Your Speech explains what you need to know, research and allow for before you start to write your speech. This includes practical issues, such as knowing how long you have, what will precede and follow your speech, and what equipment you will need or have available (e.g. a microphone); unusual situations you may need to deal with or avoid; and tips to help you develop an appropriate speech for your particular audience.

Writing Your Speech provides a basic and practical guide to speechwriting, including where to start; how and when to deal with particular situations; how to make the speech flow and keep the audience interested; how to bring your speech to a close; and how and when to use toasts.

Presentation and Delivery discusses the pros and cons of various presentation techniques, including the use of cards or notes (or even slides), and goes on to describe effective preparation. In readiness for your big day, it tells you how to minimise nerves; how to make best use of your voice and sound professional; when to pause and how to deal with unexpected problems such as a cough or hiccups, lack of audience response, or the dreaded heckler or snorer.

Dare to be Different is aimed more at the experienced speaker or presenter, although confident novice speakers may also find it useful. It provides suggestions for how to make your speech truly stand out by adopting a different format or presentation style, such as the use of video or slides.

Ten Steps to the Perfect Wedding Speech is a concise summary of all the advice offered in this book.

The extensive *Samples Library* gives sample speeches on which you can build – including several for the more unusual speech-maker, such as the bride, bridesmaid or groom's mother. Several styles are included, and most have been adapted from real-life weddings. Also provided are a wide selection of toasts for various wedding situations and some famous and apt quotes that you may like to weave into your speech.

Where to Find Out More lists some books and web sites that you may find useful in researching your topics, writing or presenting your speech.

First some advice

Before we start, let me offer one piece of advice above all others in this book. That is:

PLAN AHEAD!

Don't put off writing your speech – or reading this book, or even practising your speech – to the night before, or even the week before. Read this book as early as possible, and jot down ideas as soon as you can. Far better to have your speech written, read through and sitting in a drawer for a few weeks or months, than to be frantically scribbling amidst a mound of paper for 48 hours before the big day. Who wants to look half-asleep in the wedding photos because of late-night speech-plotting? Not you, that's for sure.

SO DO IT NOW.

Then put it away and get on with your life until two weeks before the wedding. Then, take it out and re-read it, making any changes you want. Then practise, practise, practise. THEN, and only then, can you panic about it. Now read.

Chapter 1
The Basics of Wedding Speeches

Speeches have featured at weddings for hundreds, if not thousands, of years. Formal or informal, sombre or light-hearted, they are a part of the big day that many look forward to, while others – particularly the speech-makers – often can't wait for them to be over. They are often one of the things people most clearly recall about the big occasion – not every word of course, but a good speech will be remembered as a highlight of the wedding.

Traditionally, speeches are given by men, but nowadays many women are choosing to have their say, including the bride, the groom's mother and the bridesmaids, along with others such as siblings and in some cases even the children of one or both of the happy couple. With ethnic or multi-racial weddings, the diversity of options is even greater. Here we look first at traditional wedding etiquette, outlining what is expected and the rules that must be followed particularly at formal weddings, before looking at less formal, alternative or additional speeches.

Wedding speech etiquette

This section describes traditional wedding speech etiquette for Christian or non-denominational weddings in the UK. As we discuss later in this chapter, different traditions exist for other countries and cultures, and there are often fewer speeches made at second marriages, or particularly informal or non-traditional weddings, so the information here may not be appropriate for all weddings. However, for the majority of weddings, at least some of these will apply.

When are speeches given?

Generally, if the wedding is a formal one involving a sit-down meal, speeches take place after the meal is served, often to the accompaniment of coffee and liqueurs as well as the traditional champagne. In some cases, the speeches can be given before the food instead, and this is often the case where the meal is served buffet-style or in a setting where there are other people present (such as a restaurant) or where the guests are mostly standing.

Should I stand or sit?

Traditionally, the speech-maker stands, usually behind the top table if in a formal setting, or at the front of the group if not. In situations where one or more of the speech-makers is unable to stand, all speeches may be read while seated. In such cases it is usual for the speech-makers to be seated in a raised area so as to be visible to all the guests. If the majority of the guests are standing – for example at a large, informal gathering following a small, private wedding ceremony – the speakers should also stand, again in an area visible to all those present.

Who says what?
At most 'traditional' weddings in the UK and elsewhere, the following persons are expected to make a speech, in this order:

- The father of the bride, or his equivalent
- The bridegroom
- The best man.

These three speeches are the basic 'must haves' of any formal wedding, although less formal or small-scale weddings may not require all of the above. Always check with your bride and groom what they expect before you start preparing your speech – they might prefer a light-hearted, conversational approach for their speeches rather than a stiff, etiquette-bound delivery, in which case the information in the section *Informal weddings* may be of more help to you.

When planning your speech, which is covered in the next chapter, keep in mind the main points of each speech as listed in the section *'Traditional' speeches* on page 14. This will help to avoid overlap between you and the other speech-makers, and make your speech unique yet true to tradition.

Who introduces whom?

The first of the speeches is usually introduced either by a master of ceremonies (commonly provided by the hotel, if the reception is held at one) or by the best man. Each speaker then introduces the next. Alternatively the master of ceremonies (or best man) can introduce each. Make sure you know which applies to your wedding before you write your speech.

'Traditional' speeches

Here we look at the traditional content of each of the three main speeches. Each speaker is responsible for thanking or praising certain people for their role in the wedding, so this is quite important. After all, if all three speakers say how wonderful the bridesmaids look but nobody mentions the bride's mother, you will all be in trouble!

The father of the bride

By tradition, the bride's father makes a speech that effectively hands his daughter over to her new husband. This should include both praise for the bride and good wishes for their future together, as well as some acknowledgement of the groom's family and friends of the couple. A similar but usually shorter speech along the same lines can be made by the groom's father if wished.

The main points you need to cover in this speech are:

1. A toast to the bride and bridegroom. This is the most important requirement of this speech, and is most frequently made at the end of the speech as it provides a point of closure, but you can start with it instead if you prefer. Take your pick from the selection of toasts provided later in this book.

2. Next, welcome the following (in order):
   - The groom's parents (usually by first names)
   - Other relations
   - Friends
   - Distinguished guests (for example, the vicar or priest)
   - Any others, by name if appropriate.

3. Then thank particular people by name for their help, for example the bride's mother, the caterers, the ushers, the flower-arrangers.

4. Comment favourably on the bride's appearance and demeanour, praise her past achievements and thank her for her part in family life.

5. Next, if you haven't already done so, welcome the groom into the bride's family with words of praise for his character.

6. To end, offer advice – usually light-hearted or in jest – to the happy couple and wish them well for the future.

Sometimes the bride's father may be unavailable and this speech may be performed by a 'substitute'. In this case, see *A note on substitutes* on page 19.

The bridegroom

It's your big day, so no one should expect a mammoth speech from you. You have better things to worry about. However, you will be expected to thank a few people, to praise your bride and to propose a toast to bridesmaids and pageboys (if you have them). Here are the main points for you to cover:

1. Thank the guests and previous speaker (usually the bride's father) for his good wishes.

2. Thank the bride's parents for the reception (if appropriate) and for their welcome into the family.

3. Thank your own parents for their past help in family life and your own upbringing.

4. It's optional, but one of the best ways to get in your new mother-in-law's good books is to single out her and your own mother for particular attention at this point with a few carefully chosen words of appreciation. You should give them small gifts to thank them for all their help with the wedding (flowers or a small memento, nothing particularly fancy is required). This is often followed by a toast to 'the mothers'.

5. Thank your best man and any ushers for their services. If you wish, at this point, you can add a few humorous comments about the best man, to which he can respond in kind in his own speech.

6. Praise the bride and thank her parents for the gift of their daughter. Many a bridegroom uses this point to describe how he met his new wife or how he proposed, and to tell what he thinks of her. Remember, a little romance is always welcome, but spare too much mush and gory detail.

7. Toast the bridesmaids, after naming and praising them. It is often the custom to give them small gifts of appreciation by which they can remember the occasion. Try to find something that will appeal to them personally, reflecting their own interests. It need not be expensive.

Of all the speech-makers, you will probably be the most nervous – but don't worry, this is expected. You will find some advice on how to deal with nerves in the chapter *Presentation and Delivery*. For examples of speeches given by other bridegrooms, and typical toasts to use, see the *Samples Library* later in this book.

The best man

The best man's is probably the most eagerly awaited speech, and should round off the proceedings with jollity. It is often the ideal opportunity for some good-humoured teasing of the bridegroom, although this should not be to the point of embarrassment unless you know he will take it on the chin. Keep it clear of smuttiness and questionable jokes, and particularly do not mention previous partners, except by very indirect reference ('all of his previous girlfriends' is usually acceptable; 'his former fiancée' is definitely not!). Some examples, in a variety of styles, are provided in the *Samples Library*. Here are the main points to remember:

1. If there are bridesmaids, your official duty is to speak on their behalf (unless they are speaking for themselves) and to thank the groom for his toast and gifts to them.

2. Thank the bride and groom for allowing you to be best man – often the first opportunity for a joke or anecdote – and express admiration for them, praising the bride on her appearance.

3. If there are any, read a few cards or faxes from absent guests, and tell where the rest and any gifts on display (not as common as it once was) may be seen after the meal.

4. Wish the bride and groom well in their new life together. This creates a natural break, so is the ideal place for a further toast to the bride and groom if you feel one is warranted.

5. Now is the time for the main thrust of the speech, commonly details of the groom's previous exploits, especially if you've known him since childhood. Don't forget a few words about the bride, such as when they first met or when you first met the two of them together.

6. Round it off by thanking the hosts on behalf of the wedding party, and introducing the next item (which may be a meal, if speeches are given first, or a move into another area while the tables are cleared away for dancing).

If you're not used to making speeches and are nervous at the prospect, don't try to be someone you're not. Adopt a tone and style that suits you, not what you see as a 'real' best man. It will only sound false if you don't. Some more advice on this can be found in the chapter _Presentation and Delivery_.

A note on substitutes

If the bride's father is dead, or is unable or unwilling to make the speech, it is traditional for 'his' speech to be given instead by a male relative or family friend – a godfather or favourite uncle is often chosen. These days it is not uncommon, however, for the task to be given to the bride's mother, sister or even daughter. What matters is not so much who makes the speech, but what it contains and represents.

If you are such a substitute speaker, it is normal to make

reference to the fact, but not to dwell on it. For example:

- If the bride's father is dead, say how proud he would have been, etc.

- If he is alive, but not present due to hospitalisation or illness, use similar words, but express a wish that he will soon recover (only if this is possible) or will soon be looking forward to seeing the photos, video or whatever.

- If he is present but unable to speak, acknowledge him and say you are speaking on his behalf, and you hope you do him justice. Say how pleased he is to be here today, and how it was great to see him fulfil his ambition of leading his daughter down the aisle (or whatever).

- If he and the bride's mother are divorced and not amicably, if he refused to attend or was asked not to attend, it is best not to mention him.

- If, on the other hand, he was supposed to be giving the speech but didn't make the wedding for other reasons – flight delays are a typical one – say how sorry he will have been to have missed the occasion, and how you hope you can suitably fill in for him. Act on his behalf and in his interest. For example, if no official video of the ceremony was taken, use this opportunity to ask whether anyone who recorded it for themselves could let him see a copy, as you're sure he'd love to see his daughter in all her glory. Keep it short. Don't try to improvise too much in these circumstances – everyone will appreciate that you've been subbed in at the last minute, so a few kind words about the bride will do.

Some examples of 'father of the bride' speeches are given in the *Samples Library* in this book, including several by substitutes.

Of course, substitutes may apply to other speakers – the bride may substitute for the groom if he is particularly worried about public speaking, or a friend may deputise for an ill best man, for example – but the same rules generally apply.

Other speeches

All weddings are different – how boring they would become otherwise! These days, it is not uncommon to find weddings where the 'best man' is the son or daughter of bride or groom; where the bride and groom give a joint speech; where the groom's father wishes to speak as well as the bride's, and sometimes the mothers take a turn; or where friends take on all the major roles more traditionally occupied by relations. Some even include 'theatrical' efforts by the speech-makers, such as the talented best man who sings his 'speech' cabaret-style while moving among the audience for off-the-cuff tributes to the happy couple or, more commonly, the use of visual aids to add an extra touch of humour. Brides now make speeches routinely, sometimes in place of the groom, and older bridesmaids or matrons of honour often prefer to speak for themselves rather than allowing the best man to answer a toast on their behalf. At second or late marriages in particular, children and friends of the couple tend to play important roles traditionally reserved for parents.

There are few hard-and-fast rules for such additional speeches, and even the most traditional, etiquette-laden wedding can accommodate a speech by the bride or another member of the wedding party. So if you don't occupy one of the 'traditional' roles but wish to give a speech, you will find much of the information which follows useful. You will probably find that at least one of the sample speeches suits your situation precisely or can be adapted to your own particular role.

Informal weddings

Speeches must fit in with the rest of the wedding. Whether a speech is 'acceptable' for a particular wedding will depend on the formality of the occasion and the manner in which other speeches are being given. For example, if you ploughed your way through a formal ten-minute speech at a pub reception for a couple of teenage newlyweds, you would at best be ignored and at worst be booed off. At the same wedding an account of the groom's deviant past would be welcomed with cheers, whistles and riotous applause, but such a tirade could offend staid relations at a more family-oriented, traditional 'do' following a solemn high-church wedding.

We will look further at how to judge your audience in the next chapter, but if yours is to be a less formal occasion – for example, a reception held in a public place, or a party to welcome home a couple that have been married abroad – here are some tips for you:

- Informal wedding receptions may not have a 'top table' at which the speech-makers are gathered; if this is the case, try to find somewhere that can be easily seen by all the guests and either stand or sit on a table so your voice projects across the group.

- Short speeches by several people are often more welcome than two or three longer ones. Try getting a group of the couple's friends to put a speech together in which each takes part, rather than one speech recited by a nervous best man. (This is less likely to be heckled, for a start.)

- No matter how informal, you still need to be polite and include the usual thanks. Don't forget that the informal wedding is not the norm for older people, including parents, who will still expect some semblance of tradition and acknowledgement of their hard work.

- If the atmosphere is generally humorous and light-hearted, and the venue has suitable facilities, consider one of the options discussed in the chapter *Dare to be Different*.

- If the wedding is being held abroad and you will be attending together with a handful of others, borrow or rent a camcorder a few weeks before you leave and use it to capture messages for the bride and groom from those friends and relations who won't be present. This will go a long way towards replacing a long speech and will dispel any regrets by the couple that they may have missed out by not having a large, crowded reception. On the other hand, if the speech is to be given at a reception when they return, try to get hold of some video or photos from their holiday to include as part of the speech.

- If the reception is to be held in a public area, such as a pub or restaurant where other people may overhear, keep all speeches short, friendly and clean. Don't try to include people from outside your own group, even if they heckle. The venue's management should get rid of any 'gatecrashers'.

There's one rule you mustn't forget, however informal the wedding: thank all those who deserve thanks, especially the bridesmaids, and always praise the bride – or you'll live to regret it!

Second marriages and late marriages

It is not uncommon these days for either bride or groom, or both, to have been married before. Whether divorced or widowed, or indeed if the previous liaison was annulled or never cemented in marriage, a certain amount of tact needs to be employed. Although divorce and subsequent remarriage is becoming more widely accepted, as is long-term cohabitation (living together without being married), many people still find the concept difficult to relate to or recognise. In any case, you should not assume that everyone present will know of the previous relationship; older generations of the new partner's family in particular may not have been told.

Whatever the circumstances, references to previous partners in a speech would normally be considered in bad taste – although where one or both parties are widowed it is not totally unknown to make brief mention of the previous spouse.

Most of the sample speeches given in this book are equally suited to first and subsequent marriages, including weddings that take place late in life or late in a relationship (for example, where the couple already have children), but there are often subtle differences in the way the speeches as a whole are conducted, particularly if the couple are older and thus not still under the control of parents:

- The bride's father might not make a speech, particularly if his daughter has been previously married, or if he does, it is often not much more than a toast.

- There might not be a best man, particularly if the wedding party is small or the ceremony was held in a register office.
- There might not be bridesmaids or pageboys.

As a result, there are usually only two, short speeches:

- A toast to bride and groom, usually made by a male friend of the couple, or the best man, if there is one.
- The bridegroom's response.

In each case the tone is usually slightly more formal and less jokey than for first marriages, particularly with older couples who may have been previously widowed.

However, these are not hard-and-fast rules, only the norm. Some second marriages, and marriages that occur many years into a relationship, exude fun and laughter at every opportunity – it all depends on the character of your bride and groom. To ensure your speech is suitable, always ask your bride or groom for details of who will be attending and who will be speaking, before you start to write your own words.

The existing children, if any, of the bride and/or groom should always be acknowledged, and this is especially important if they are young and still living at home. The marriage or remarriage of their parent can be a difficult time for them, although this is not always obvious, and welcoming them into the new family with words of praise can help to alleviate this and make them feel more at home.

Traditions for other faiths and cultures

This is a difficult area to cover fully, as there are so many faiths, cultures and combinations of each to consider. Most 'established' religions and cultures place great emphasis on the wedding as a social and cultural occasion, and each has its own rules, procedures and traditions for speeches. For example:

- At Jewish weddings the bridegroom traditionally speaks last, and the bride is not expected to speak at all.

- In the US, the best man usually makes the first speech, followed by the groom, and the father of the bride rarely speaks at all.

- At traditional Irish weddings it's almost a free-for-all, with anyone who wishes to give a short speech or propose a toast given the floor to do so.

- At Hindi weddings there are usually no formal speeches other than a welcome speech beforehand, but this is usually made by the person conducting the ceremony.

If you are attending a wedding where one or more of the participants is of a faith or culture other than your own, make sure you ask them for guidance before you start to plan your speech. While a light-hearted comment on how the bride spent her teenage years might be acceptable to your own friends and family, it might well be considered offensive to those of a particularly strong or moral faith or whose native culture frowns upon such acts. Lurid descriptions of boozy student nights with the groom may not go down too well if many of the bride's relations are teetotal. Make sure you know what to expect and what is acceptable for the particular situation before you start. Some books and web sites that you may find useful are listed in *Where to Find Out More* on page 149.

General guidance for all speeches

The following rules and guidance apply to all speeches and all situations:

- Keep it short – between two and eight minutes. Trim your first effort down ruthlessly. Guests rarely complain that a speech is too short, but we all know when one is too long.

- Stand while giving your speech, unless you've agreed beforehand that all speeches will be made sitting down.

- Don't fidget, hop about from one foot to another, scratch or fiddle. Hold something (your wineglass or notes, for example) to help avoid this. You will find tips on this in the chapter *Presentation and Delivery*.

- Don't swear or use words that only part of the audience will understand (slang, street-talk or foreign expressions).

- Don't offer political or religious opinions.

- Don't use racist, sexist or other potentially offensive jokes or anecdotes.

- Don't degrade or tease anyone, even in jest – the groom is the exception, if you're the best man, but even he should not be made to squirm too much.
- Don't refer to past arguments or differences, or previous relationships.
- If you're a serious person, don't try to be too funny. It won't work. Be yourself.
- Don't try to be clever – it rarely works and will alienate your listeners.
- Don't get drunk beforehand, and don't smoke while speaking.
- Always test any equipment (microphones, projectors, etc.) beforehand. Make sure you know how to switch it on and off.
- If you make notes or use cards, take at least two copies and give one copy to another guest beforehand, in case of loss or accident. Number all pages clearly in case you drop them.

Chapter 2
Planning Your Speech

Planning a speech sounds simple – surely you just follow a set of rules? Unfortunately not: there are no hard-and-fast rules on the content of wedding speeches, as we have already seen, and there are similarly no rules for how to plan, write or deliver your speech. What this book can do is give you suggestions, and some guidance on what to consider, plus some examples of good speeches from which you can get some ideas. After that it's up to you!

So where to start? Well, let's look first at *you*.

Why me?

This is the first question to consider. Indeed, you are probably already asking yourself this very thing. Why have you been chosen to speak at this wedding? Is it because you are a close friend or relative of the bride/groom? Is it because you are wise and can give sage advice on life? Is it because you are a humorous, outgoing person? Knowing this can give you an idea about what to say in your speech, and what people probably *expect* you to say.

What will I talk about?

This depends on your role: as the bride's father you're usually expected to talk about your daughter; as the groom, about how you met; as the best man, about the groom's past life. However, there's no reason why you can't include a few stories about something or someone else, as long as it's relevant to the wedding.

While researching topics for your speech, talk to close family and friends for ideas and anecdotes. Note that asking once doesn't always guarantee success – keep at it. Be persistent, although not annoyingly so. If after several attempts you're not getting much response, try someone else. For example, the groom might not want to tell you much that's of use, but his parents, brothers or even schoolfriends might. One great way to get people to talk freely about a subject is over a meal or drink – when they are relaxed.

What will it be like?

The main factor that will determine the tone and type of speech that you deliver is the *style* of the wedding you are attending – is it going to be a very formal, religious ceremony with hundreds of distant relations, or a quick trip to the nearest register office with a handful of friends? Knowing this will help to narrow down the possibilities and only when this is done can you write an effective, acceptable speech. So you must first *know your audience*. Then there are a few things you need to investigate, depending on your particular role.

Know your audience

Don't get me wrong: I don't mean you need to know them all personally. There are basically two things you need to know:

- What tone to set
- What topics to mention or avoid.

In order to write a speech that your audience will appreciate and to which they will relate, you need a general picture of the 'average' guest. Don't assume that you know this already: you might well know a number of people that are going to the wedding, but are they representative of the whole guest-list?

This is a trap the best man, in particular, often falls into. By basing his speech around gags and anecdotes that his friends will find funny, he may well offend, confuse or shock other guests. Similarly, the groom may assume that his easy-going, up-for-anything relations will appreciate family 'in-jokes', but will they mean anything to his bride's relations, or their friends? The bride may well be a sassy young thing with body-piercings and raucous friends who keep her out till the small hours, but her family could be devoutly religious and the ceremony equally so. Will your one-liners work on them, or will they be received in a stony, disapproving silence? Then again, with weddings whose guest-list is full of twenty-somethings, the problem swings the other way: don't, whatever you do, make your speech stuffy and formal – it'll go down like the proverbial lead balloon and you're likely to suffer as a result!

So how do you get to know your audience? There's really only one way: talk to the major players in the wedding party and ask them who is coming. Find out a bit about each family (or the other family, if yours is involved) and the friends who will be attending. What is the balance of numbers between family and friends? What is the approximate average age? Are they mostly business types or country folk? Are they in their mid-fifties or younger? Are there many young children attending? And so on.

From this you should be able to judge the tone of your speech. As an additional precaution against last-minute changes, ask a representative of each family to keep you up-to-date on any serious illnesses or bereavements in the family, or any change to the 'cast list', so you can make or remove reference to the people concerned ahead of time.

How do I avoid upsetting anyone?

Make sure to find out in advance about any potentially awkward or upsetting situations that may affect your choice of jokes or anecdotes. This comes down mainly to knowing your audience – if you skipped this bit go back now!

There is the age-old problem of family skeletons – and I don't mean skinny old Aunt Sue, bag of bones that she is. Now there, you see. How do you know that Aunt Sue isn't ill? Maybe she suffers from an eating disorder or wasting disease. Maybe she is naturally slim, but wishes she wasn't – or at least wishes people would stop talking about it. She may laugh at jokes about her figure, but you should consider that they may be hurtful – even if not to her, to her family. They are best avoided.

Every family has its black sheep, its tragic story, its unresolved argument and its broken marriage; all often brushed under the rug so firmly that you may know nothing about it at all. To avoid giving offence, don't make jokes or tell funny stories that make reference to death, illness, divorce or separation, family feuds or sibling rivalry. There are other, less obvious pitfalls: the mention of 'the patter of tiny feet' is often made with the best intentions, but could upset if the couple or guests have problems with fertility; similarly, mentions of the bride 'leaving home' are nonsensical if the couple have been cohabiting before marriage, or if either has a child from a past relationship, and may cause embarrassment.

There are subjects that, to my mind, should be banned from all wedding speeches, even when used in jest. These include:

- Divorce or separation – you'd be surprised how many wedding speeches mention them.

- Illness – other than a brief mention of an invited guest who is ill. Jokes about cancer, etc. aren't funny, especially to someone whose mother or partner is suffering from it.

- Religious differences – by all means celebrate the religion of the wedding party, but not to the detriment of other religious groups: even if the wedding party are all of one faith, don't assume all the guests are.

- Politics – don't even think about it.
- Family feuds and sibling rivalry – no matter how close a family appears, there's always some hidden dispute.
- Past mistakes and bad relationship decisions.
- Death – obviously.

Some people would add sex to this list, but this rather depends on the audience – many, whatever their age group, will expect a few smutty references or a risqué toast from the best man.

Don't impose your own opinions on your guests. For example, don't go on at length about the 'dreadful' rate of divorce or opine about its increase being due to couples 'not trying hard enough'. No matter what your own personal view, there are probably people in your audience who are going through, or have been through, a painful divorce or troubled marriage, and this could upset them. Similarly, don't use your speech as a platform for other points not related to the bride and groom. Your aim is not to rally the troops or make a political statement, nor to espouse the values of knowing your God: it's to celebrate the happy couple and propose their health and happiness. Do this, sit down and shut up!

Know the competition

All right, so you're not really in competition with your fellow speech-makers, but if you've all used the same speechwriting book (hopefully this one!), you're likely to be competing for the same gags – or even if not, you may relate the same anecdote about the bride or her groom. Communication is essential. Imagine how you would panic if the speaker before you used all your best material – or said something that totally contradicted it!

Make sure your speeches don't clash by all agreeing beforehand about what you each will cover, with each person picking a particular subject to leave to the others. This helps to avoid the prospect of three speeches that all tell the same story of how Bob and Julie met – embarrassing for the speech-makers (especially the final one, who frantically wracks his or her brains for an alternative) and extremely tedious and disappointing for the audience.

It might not always be possible to co-ordinate all the speeches, but you are sure to know at least one other person who is giving a speech, so you can minimise the risk of duplication: if you're the best man, you must know the groom, so you can at least discuss brief details of areas to cover. The father of the bride is often the odd-man-out here, but by sticking to stories about his daughter can usually avoid too much commonality with the others. Brides and bridesmaids tend to take a different angle if speaking anyway, so are unlikely to suffer too much from this problem, but it's always a good idea to have a spare joke or story to refer to if someone else nabs your best one.

Know your limits

As well as limits of taste or decency, which we pretty much covered earlier on, you need to be aware of the limits of your surroundings and the inevitable limits on time. Consider the following questions:

1. Where do I fit in?
   - Will I be introduced? By whom?
   - What will be happening immediately before my speech? Are there toasts to which I need to reply?
   - Who will speak after me (if anyone)? Do I need to introduce the next speaker?
   - If I am the last speaker, do I need to explain what happens next? If so, what does happen next?
   - Will I have time to freshen up between the meal and my speech?

2. How long do I have?
   - Is there a minimum time as well as a maximum? If so, what is it?
   - How long are the other speeches likely to be? It's best to get them all roughly the same length, although a minute here or there is not important.

- If mine is the last speech, people may be getting restless. How can I prevent this from becoming a problem?

3. Where will I be?
   Investigate this thoroughly, particularly the following points:
   - Will I have to stand or sit? In most cases you will be expected to stand, but if one of the speakers is unable to, or if the event is small and intimate, it is not unusual for all speeches to be given while seated.
   - Will there be any background noise that I need to speak over? (For example, the noise of traffic if windows are open, or the noisy children of guests can be very distracting, but you can plan for them if need be.)
   - Will there be lights shining on me, in my eyes or between the guests and me? If so, could they be redirected? For example, spotlights are easy to move in advance; chandeliers are not – it's easier to move yourself in this case. This point is particularly important if you intend using visual aids.
   - Will I have a place to stand notes or cue cards (if using)?
   - If using a microphone (see below), will it stand on the table or floor? Will it be passed to me or be there already?

4. How will I be heard?
   - Will I require a microphone in order that all guests can hear me clearly? If you're not sure, go to the venue, preferably at a similar time of day to when you will be

speaking, and get a friend to judge from the back and sides of the room – remembering that the room will be full of people on the day. Open windows and doors to check for background noise.

- If a microphone seems preferable, is one available? Will I have to hold it or will it have a stand – if so, is it adjustable? How does it switch on and off?
- Will I require any additional equipment or props? Will there be power points suitably located for any such equipment?
- Will I have time to practise with the microphone/ equipment on the day? If not, can I practise beforehand? If you are unfamiliar with microphones, this is highly recommended, to avoid problems with feedback, etc.

What to do next

By now you should have a good idea of:

- Whom you are addressing and how they are likely to respond
- When and where you fit in to the wedding schedule
- What sticky subjects to avoid and what you mustn't forget to include
- How long you need to speak for and whether you will need a microphone.

Now you need to sit down and work out what you want to say.

Chapter 3
Writing Your Speech

This chapter covers the two main aspects of speechwriting: the content of a good speech, and the practicalities of writing a speech. The first provides a basic and practical guide to putting a speech together, including how to start; how and when to deal with particular situations and when to use jokes, quotes and toasts; how to make the speech flow and keep the audience interested; and, importantly, how to end. It should tell you all you need to structure the ideal speech. The second part of the chapter then suggests how to go about writing it.

For further ideas, look at the speeches, toasts and quotes in the *Samples Library* later in the book.

All speeches, whatever they are about, need a start, a middle and an end. Here are some suggestions for each.

Getting a good start

First impressions count. Particularly with a speech. If you fluff the start, you're on to a loser – unless you manage to make a joke out of it and thus turn it to your advantage.

First, the niceties:

- Address your guests as 'Ladies and gentlemen' or less formally with 'Hello everyone' if you prefer – whichever seems most suitable to the occasion. Avoid naming specific people (e.g. 'Bob, Angela, Mum and Dad, family and friends') – it sounds false and you're bound to forget someone! However, if you have distinguished guests, such as a priest, rabbi or other celebrant, it is acceptable to mention them; for example, 'Ladies, gentlemen, Reverend Jones.'

- Introduce yourself, unless it's obvious – if you're the bridegroom you don't need to bother, as they *should* all know who you are by now, but while the guests may be able to point out the best man, they might not know whether you're the groom's brother, cousin or a friend. It's good to let them know. This is also particularly important if you're a substitute for, say, the bride's father. If so, read the section on substitutes on page 19.

- If you have a toast to reply to, do so before starting the main speech.

Now the difficult bit; your real 'opening line'. Here are a few ideas. You can find others in the *Samples Library*.

- Refer to a book (this one will do!). Tell the audience 'I know nothing about speeches, so I've read this book from cover to cover. And, as it says on page 39 ... [open at marked page, look blank, then panicked.] Oh no. Wrong book.' This usually gets a laugh and is also a great way to hide a crib sheet. If you do get lost during your speech, each time you open the book you'll raise another laugh (as long as you don't do it *too* often) and, more importantly, you'll get to read your notes.

- Find a link between the year the bride (if you're her father or groom) or groom (if you're his father or the best man) was born, and key events or people in that year. Make a joke or compliment out of the connection. For example, if your guests enjoy a drink or two: 'Do you know, the year Jane was born, England won the World Cup. So my wife allowed me two hangovers that year. And by tomorrow, I'll probably have another.' Or, setting a more serious tone: 'Over the years, a lot of people have asked me why we called our son Martin. It was because he was born a week after the death of Martin Luther King. Jolene and I hoped for our son to grow up fighting for the principles that great man taught. And I'm pleased to say he has.'

- Use a short anecdote about the bride or groom to get the audience on your side. One from childhood usually goes down well. For example, 'When Jane was two, she got her head stuck up the chimney while looking for Santa Claus. We had to get the fire brigade to get her out, you know. And now she's marrying a fireman three weeks before Christmas.

Thank goodness for that.' Don't, however, use a joke – it's too clichéd and you run the risk of no one laughing – and that spells disaster.

- If nothing else quite fits, use a quote. It is somewhat clichéd to start a speech this way, but not so much so as to be unacceptable. For example: 'Lord Tennyson once said, "A happy bridesmaid makes a happy bride." Well, last year Jane was bridesmaid to her sister Polly, and their smiles lit up the whole church. And just look at her now.' Some suitable quotes are given at the back of this book. If, on reading back your speech, you find the quotation sounds too pretentious, try moving or adding a sentence before it so it's not your initial line. That often helps.

Now you can move on from your first lines – always the most difficult – and get into the swing of your speech. Make sure you've got all the thank-yous, etc. out of the way before you dive into the bulk of it – unless there are too many, in which case you may prefer to split them between the beginning and end of the speech.

A few words about jokes

Before we go any further, a few words about jokes. Most of us will have had to sit uncomfortably through a speech given by someone who thought he was funny but wasn't. We've all watched the novice 'comic' after-dinner speaker or the party bore whose 'act' dies on its feet. It's embarrassing to the point of pain. So let's face it: some people are natural joke-tellers, others are not. You cannot make an unfunny guy funny, no matter how hard you try. As Frank Carson so succinctly put it: 'It's the way I tell 'em.'

So if you are not generally a joker, if you always forget the punchline or your attempts at humour generally fall flat, don't be tempted to overdo it in your speech. People may expect a certain amount of humour, particularly from the best man, but they'd rather *no* jokes than badly told jokes. There is usually room for one or two one-liners, though, in any speech.

If you're unsure whether your jokes will work, keep these points in mind:

- The best jokes are short ones. Stick to one-liners: don't leave people wondering where you're going with it.
- Don't try and adapt someone else's jokes to suit the situation. It doesn't work. If you want to make a joke personal, use your own. Otherwise just lift it in its entirety.
- Racist, religionist, sexist, political and dirty (adult) jokes are OUT. So are mother-in-law jokes.
- Old jokes aren't necessarily bad jokes. At least your audience will recognise them as jokes!
- Try jokes out on family and/or friends beforehand. Get them to tell you, honestly, whether they are funny, and whether

you are telling them the right way. Children are particularly honest in such situations (brutally so).

If you can't think of your own, there are numerous jokes and funny stories you can use in the books listed in *Where to Find Out More* on page 149.

The middle bit

Once the start is out of the way, you're effectively heading for the middle of your speech. And what do you expect when you get there? Hmm. Many people forget this bit. They concentrate solely on getting the start and finish right, and hope this will get them through. This is no way to structure a good speech. Your audience should be able to judge where you are in your speech, so the end doesn't come as a sudden shock. (After all, if you're really worried about half the audience falling asleep, you can at least give the others a clue when to dig them in the ribs before you announce the toast!)

Think of your speech as a gentle mountain that you have to climb. Indeed, you may already view it as such, although probably with less of the gentle! Start out firmly, establishing a good pace. Not too fast, not too slow. Climb steadily towards the peak (the middle of your speech), stay there for a short while and look around, then stride back down the other side to the end.

If nothing else, this analogy will give you something to aim at if you're nervous: once you've passed the middle mark you're on the home straight and can relax – but don't race along or you'll trip yourself up.

So what characterises the middle of a speech?

For a start, your audience should be relaxed. You've set the tone with your opening lines, and have got most of the essential stuff – the thank-yous and so forth – out of the way. They know you're not going to produce a total dog's dinner, because you've got this far OK. They are likely to be reclining with a large glass, particularly if yours is not the first speech, and wish to be entertained.

Now you can move into those longer jokes or anecdotes. Don't wander off at tangents, but indulge a little in the telling of the tale. Embellish it a bit. Use adjectives (descriptive words) to enhance the visual impression of your narrative – or, if you wish, use visual aids (a great way to wake up a dozing audience – see the next chapter on *Presentation and Delivery*). Let's see what a difference a few adjectives and a bit of embellishment can make.

Here's an extract from a rather dull speech, about a rather dull student (now the bridegroom) who discovers there's more to life than study…

'When John first went to university, he didn't know anyone. Because he was shy, he went to lectures alone for ages. Then he

bought himself a second-hand car, and as he was the only student with one and the nearest town was ten miles away, suddenly people wanted to know him. So he started going out with girls and going to parties and became much more confident.'

Now for a little embellishment to help the audience really see what you're talking about. Try reading this aloud, giving it lots of emphasis and expression:

'When our hero first ventured out to the big wide world of uni, he hid himself away. He crept furtively to lectures and sat at the back. He avoided girls and boys alike; he spoke to nobody. He was shy. [Turn to the audience with a sad face. Expect "ahs" from audience and a kick from the groom.] But … all was not lost. His salvation came in the form of a rusty, foul-smelling Ford Escort. It was ancient: held together with chewing gum and rubber bands, it ate up his grant and it drove like a tank. But to a bunch of skint and stranded students it was as good as a limo. Girls flocked to it like kids round an ice-cream van and, overnight, John became popular! And you know, he suddenly found there was more to life than medical books, and soon he started indulging in 'hands-on' study … especially with girls! Soon he'd evolved into the party animal we all know and love, and it's just as well … otherwise he'd never have been interesting enough to attract Paula, and we wouldn't be here today.'

See how the second version gives much more of a visual impression than the first. You can almost picture the shy college boy and his stinking, noisy motor (if you've been a student, it's not that hard to imagine!), and see how that very thing helped him to get in with the 'in crowd' and move on in life. Don't worry if your tale is not entirely factual – don't make it up entirely, but overemphasising the state of the car, for example, is designed to raise a laugh, not be 100 per cent accurate. So what if it had a full MOT? Who cares! This is called poetic licence and all the best speech-makers use it.

Keep anecdotes relatively short – but not too short so they become a list. The one just given is about 170 words. Much more than 200 without introducing a new angle and your audience will start to lose interest. Much less than 50 and they will not grasp the point before you move on. Always leave a pause of a couple of seconds between anecdotes or subjects so that your audience realises you have come to the end.

A few words about difficult situations

Somewhere between the beginning and the middle part of your speech is often where you have to explain away some unusual or difficult situation. For example, in the case of step-parents, who is married to whom – there may be more than one 'father' and 'mother' figure attending for each side – or why someone usually expected to speak is not doing so. You might have to announce a bereavement that not all the guests will have known of before the wedding, or even warn guests of a potential problem with the evening's entertainment or – worse – the catering.

Whatever the awkward situation, look first at whether you really need to mention it at all. Some things are better left for guests to find out for themselves – the step-parents being one good example, unless they insist upon it. As usual, it depends on the families involved. If the split has been recent and one party finds it difficult, it is best to gloss over the situation. If the split occurred some years ago and each partner is now happy with the situation, then you can probably include some introductions. But it is generally best to keep them short.

The situations that you *can't* avoid mentioning are often last-minute changes that you wouldn't be aware of yet. So we'll discuss these in the next chapter.

You might be asked by someone to include a mention of a particular person in your speech. For example, an uncle who has recently died after a long illness. Think carefully before you accept. It is often the case that a brief mention, followed by a toast to absent friends, does not derail the happy occasion. However, if feelings in the family are still raw, it may be better not to mention the person by name, or, depending on your position, to leave the job to someone closer to the person concerned (but discuss it with them first). If you think such a mention is likely to change the mood of the guests, or cast a shadow over proceedings, don't do it. If this is the case, explain tactfully to the person who asked you and if they disagree, ask them to discuss it with other members of the family for their opinions.

Rounding it off well

Don't let your speech drag on and on. If, once you've written it, you find it takes longer than about eight minutes to read it at a slow pace, cut it down ruthlessly. There's always one joke or funny story that you can cut out without affecting the flow of the rest of the speech, and you don't have to cover every year of the subject's life. Don't try to fit more in and make yourself speak faster – it will just confuse people.

So how do you draw to a close?

With most speeches other than wedding speeches, you would be summarising what you've previously said, refocusing the audience's minds on the subjects you've covered. You can adopt a similar style here. For example:

'So, ladies and gentlemen, we've now all seen what a wonderful girl John has taken on as his wife. A loyal, gentle, and tender-hearted one with the ability to make us all laugh. Of course, I could tell you a few horror stories as well. Who couldn't? But they would be few, as I'm sure you have gathered by now. Anyway, I'll leave it to Stuart to tell the funny stories. Meanwhile, I'd like to formally welcome John into our family – she may be inheriting your name but she'll always be our

daughter and you our son – and ask him to take good care of her, as I know he will. And finally, I would like you all to join me in a toast to the bride and groom.'

From the first line of this extract, the audience can tell the speech is coming to a close. The words 'we've … seen' and 'by now' hint that the speaker has said all he wishes to on the matter of Jane, and his later reference to the best man indicates that he wishes to move on. By pausing at the end of each sentence, the speaker draws the end out a little, giving the guests a chance to anticipate the closing toast.

Toasts

Toasts are a very traditional part of a wedding. Indeed, the whole purpose of speeches at a wedding is really to propose toasts. The speeches themselves have just developed and expanded into more of a storytelling over the years, and now simply to propose a toast without a supporting speech might seem rude. But toasts are certainly not obsolete. And just as well: they are particularly useful at both breaking up and ending speeches. They can provide a natural break in proceedings if you have just gone through a long list of thank-yous. They provide a quick and easy way to express extra thanks to particular members of the wedding party – the bride's and groom's mothers in particular are often toasted, to their apparent surprise – and if you are giving out gifts, toasts allow for the exchange to be handled without the usual accompanying dilemma of whether to applaud. And, as Mitch Murray, that famously talented speechwriter, says: 'A toast is a brilliant device; it flatters an ego, it closes a speech and it gives you an excuse to have a drink!'

So how does one propose a toast? Well, it's simple. Just say something along the lines of:

'And now, ladies and gentlemen, would you all please rise [or, *please charge your glasses*] *and join me in a toast to the happy couple.'*

The guests should then stand; at which point you hold up your glass (usually of champagne) and recite your selected toast, or simply say 'The bride and groom'. To which they will reply in kind and you all drink.

And it's really as simple as that! Particularly as I've done the hard work for you and placed some particularly apt toasts in the *Samples Library* in this book.

So now you know *what* to write, let's look at *how* to write it.

The practicalities of writing a speech

How do you write a speech? Well, as usual, there's no fixed way to do it. The following are some suggestions. The only guarantee I can give is that you will have to write and rewrite it several times before you're happy with it. So start with a pad of paper, or preferably a word processor, if you have access to one – it's much easier to swap bits in and out and change the order, and you won't have to decipher your own scrawl!

Don't bother with index cards at this stage; if you feel the need, you can transcribe your speech on to them later. At this point we want to get the main points down and flesh them out a little.

The outline

Before you start writing sentences, create an outline of what you want to cover. Use the lists in *The Basics of Wedding Speeches* and the sample speeches to put this together. It should be a simple list of topics, nothing more. For example, an outline for the father of the bride might look like this:

> Thank guests for coming
> Toast to absent friends
> Jane as a child
> Teenage years – school – dancing etc.
> University and work (briefly)
> When Jane met John
> Bit about John
> Toast to bride and groom

Or for the bridegroom:

> *Thank— **Bob** for toast—Bob and Angie for reception—*
> ***Mum and Dad** for help*
> *Jane is great because ... (toast?)*
> *Our hopes*
> *Now over to Stuart ...*
> ***Thank guests** for gifts and for coming*
> *Toast to **bridesmaids** (give presents)*
> *Sit down!*

Or the best man:

> *Reply for bridesmaids*
> *Compliment Jane's mum (Angie) and John's (Audrey) —*
> *give bouquets*
> *Duties of best man — bridesmaids, ribbing of groom,*
> *what an honour, etc.*
> *About John*
> *＊ known since school*
> *＊ first girlfriend (nerves, trousers)*
> *＊ time at uni (first weeks, the band, exams)*
> *＊ meeting Jane*
> *Few words about Jane*
> *Friends here today, absent friends (read 3 cards/faxes)*
> *Toast to bride and groom*
> *What happens next (NB: check with Jane)*

Notice how the last of the examples above is a little more detailed than the others. Here the best man has jotted down ideas for each topic. This is a good idea as you will probably think of things while developing your outline that you might forget about later. You can always cross out anything that you find you can't develop further. A good outline like this makes the rest of the process much easier!

A few words about ad libbing

The outline, as just shown, is really the basis of your speech. If you know your subject well, and you are a confident speaker – one that can ad lib at will – a good outline may well be all you need: use it as a memory aid and expand on it verbally, rather than writing every word down. It's advisable to give it a few practice runs (see the advice in the next chapter), including at least one in front of someone else, in order to iron out any difficulties.

If you're not confident enough to do this – and most of us aren't – read on.

The first draft

Now to the nitty-gritty. Working from your outline, start by writing a first sentence for each point. Don't worry about getting it perfect yet; just develop some ideas. The next few sections of this chapter will help you. If you find this too hard, first go back to your outline and try to develop it further, adding a couple of points under each listed item. Search the sample speeches and toasts for suitable phrases if you like, or refer to other books and web sites (a list is provided on page 149). Try to use mostly your own words though, or the speech will sound very manufactured – and you'll be less able to remember it.

Once you have a first sentence, review what you have and change the order of sections if necessary. Then write a further sentence. Keep going like this until you have each section covered with several sentences. Read it back to yourself and you'll probably find you add in bits and pieces as you go along. In this way, you build your speech naturally. When you think you're finished, put it away for a couple of days. When you take it out again, you're ready for draft two.

A few words about thanks

This is important! When writing your speech, make sure that the long list of thank-yous doesn't sound too much like an acceptance speech. You aren't receiving an award – you are extending the hand of friendship and acknowledging various people's contributions to the big day. Keep in mind how tedious some of those BAFTA and Oscar acceptance speeches can be, especially when they include long lists of tearful thank-yous to, or anecdotes about, people the rest of us don't know! Also, the more people you thank, the less each one seems to mean. Remember, you can always go out there after the speeches and thank particular people in person, which often means a lot more to them. Stick to brief acknowledgements of the main participants only, with the occasional nod to those that others may also wish to thank (such as the caterers, if they've done a particularly good job).

The next draft
Here we are again. But this time, you're a lot further along. You now have the basis of your speech written. Now all you need to do is flesh it out a little more, maybe move a few sections around, and check that you have the basic structure.

On reading back your part-written speech after its few days in the drawer, you might think, 'Lord, that's dreadful!' Don't despair. Some parts of it probably are. Few people get it right first time. Identify the bits you like the least, and rewrite them. Use a different joke, or scrap that quote altogether. Be ruthless. If you've started early enough, you've plenty of time to chop and change. But don't be too hard on yourself. Remember all those people who do it at the last minute – some of them have made truly terrible speeches, so yours is probably much better than that.

Before we go any further, let me say a few words about grammar.

A *few words about grammar*

As I have said on other topics in this book, the most important thing to remember in writing a speech is to be yourself. Don't be funny if you're not; and similarly, don't try to use fancy language if you normally speak quite plainly. It will sound awkward, and you are more likely to trip yourself up. There is nothing wrong with basic, simple language: just ask the Campaign for Plain English. The clearest way of saying anything is usually both the simplest and the best. Follow these rules and you'll be OK:

- Remember, your main aim is to be understood. Don't use fancy words in order to sound clever. You won't.

- Write as you speak normally. If you feel that your speech is usually too coarse, or not formal enough, try to improve it gradually. Make sure to leave out any rude words, for example, but don't bother changing I'm to I am or we won't to we will not – you will just sound stilted.

- Other than when you are trying to set a scene (see the example in *The middle bit*), avoid using two words where you could use one, or too many bland adjectives that add little value, like 'very' or 'quite'. For example: 'Now I am quite sure that we should all like to thank the chefs as well as all the other hotel staff for that really wonderful meal, which was quite delicious' could just as easily be reduced to 'And many thanks to the hotel for such a delicious meal'.

59

Practise and revise

You may think you have your speech perfectly written, but when you are practising you might find you keep tripping up on the same word. If so, don't keep practising it – change it! If there are words or names you *need* to use that you find difficult to say, first try to find an easier alternative. If, for example, you constantly get the first names of the groom's parents wrong or muddled, use 'Mr and Mrs' instead. If you can't get the punchline of the joke exactly right, change the joke. If there is no getting rid of that difficult but essential word, then there's nothing for it but practice. However, try changing the sentence around it first – leading into the problem word another way often does the trick.

The final version

Once you've practised and revised your speech to death, you are ready to put it away again. You are also ready to decide how you want to read it on the big day. Do you want to memorise it, read it, or write some notes you can glance at? The first is often too difficult; the second works only if you are used to reading to an audience and don't spend the entire speech with your head buried in the paper rather than looking at your guests. The third is what suits most of us, and this is what we will discuss in the next chapter.

Chapter 4
Presentation and Delivery

This chapter describes presentation techniques, including the use of cards or notes; how to minimise nerves; how to project your voice and/or use equipment such as microphones to best effect; when to pause; and how to deal with unexpected problems such as a cough or hiccups, lack of audience response, or the dreaded heckler or snorer.

Getting ready for the big day
Everyone prepares differently, but here are a few tips that seem to work for the majority.

Read or memorise?
Your speech is likely to be several minutes long. It is difficult for most of us to memorise anything that lengthy and to recall it perfectly on a day when we are likely to be quite nervous. Those with public speaking experience may be able to do so, but most of us will require something to jog the memory occasionally.

There is, of course, the option of reading your speech word-for-word from a written script. But this is not recommended, as you will tend to bury your nose in the paper and speak towards the table rather than the guests. Your eyes will be occupied with the reading, and your hands with the holding, so you will be unable to act expressively and animatedly. You will quite likely isolate and bore your audience. Imagine yourself in their place: it would be like going to the theatre and the actors reading their lines from a book! But if you have no alternative – for example, if you are standing in for someone who's taken ill at the last moment, or if you have problems with your memory – people will understand. Just try to look up and smile occasionally, and not to race through it. Make a joke of it if possible, to keep the audience on your side.

The ideal solution is to create yourself a set of brief notes, on cue cards or a single sheet of paper. Use coloured pens (or **bold** or *italic,* if using a computer) and larger type to highlight important words or names, to help guide your eye to them at an appropriate moment. Indent or number items in lists so you can jump straight back to the right one. If using cards, number them or tie them together – and take a copy in case your original version gets lost. If you're thinking of using paper, I suggest instead a piece of cardboard – paper can flop about and this will distract the audience, as well as making you less confident of your place.

Below are some examples of cue cards:

WELCOME
Hi everybody: My name's Stuart
First I've some people to thank:
    Joe for speech, toast (joke: first time Joe has
    made toast since college)
    Gail's parents (John and Jane) –
    reception and welcome
    Joe's dad (Artie) – speech and stag night
PAUSE

TOP 3 BEST MEN TO HAVE ... AND NOT HAVE
Clint Eastwood (nobody wanted to refuse)
Rory Bremner (guest impressions)
David Beckham (well, he is the best...)
    Peter Stringfellow (too keen on the girls)
    Robbie Williams (too popular with the girls)
    Anyone too good-looking. **Except me**

> *JOE AT COLLEGE*
> *Fresher's – 24 societies inc.* **astrophysics** *– to meet "brainy birds"*
> *First year – beer, birds, not many books.* **SHOW SLIDE**
> *Second year – the band, exams* **SLIDE 2**
> *Third year – hard work, panic, "stardom", finals*
>   *Passed. SOMEHOW!!*
>
> *Then he went to work.* **SLIDE 3**

Whatever you decide to do about reading your speech, be sure to rehearse it thoroughly. Rehearse it first from your full script. But don't just practise by reading your speech to yourself. Read it aloud. Read in a way that's going to reflect how you're going to have to say it to the audience. Next, try it in front of your mum, or someone else who'll give you an honest opinion of your jokes. Time it, to make sure it's not too long: if it is, edit until it's more suitable. Then write your cue cards, if you're using them, or commit the speech to memory. Then rehearse it again, from the cards/memory. And again and again until you are sick of it and recite it in your sleep. That should be about right.

If you have the opportunity, and you haven't already done so, visit the venue and try out your speech (or part of it), particularly noticing any echoes, disturbing noises from other rooms or traffic, etc. If you will be using a microphone, ask to test it out. Take a friend and stand them at the back of the room to see whether you really need the mike, and if so, that you are not shouting into it. All this will help reduce your nerves on the day, by making the surroundings feel a little more familiar.

Here are some points to note when practising. They concern your delivery of the speech, which is all important on the big day, and may not come naturally if you are not used to this kind of public speaking. Practising and being aware of them now will help you to deliver them automatically, no matter how nervous you may be. It may seem a drag, but remember, if you take the time to become comfortable with the words you're going to say, your speech will improve dramatically.

Breathe!

This sounds obvious, and you are unlikely to have trouble breathing while practising, but sometimes you might on the day, if you're particularly nervous. You'll find you're holding your breath, or trying to say too much in one breath. You might start feeling faint. The answer to all these lies in effective breathing preparation. Learn to breathe naturally, note where pauses naturally occur in your speech and use them to refill your lungs – unobtrusively mind, not in huge gulps. Try to pace yourself according to when you need to breathe, rather than rushing a few sentences to get them in before you pass out from lack of breath. We will look further at breathing in the section on delivering your speech.

Slow down!

There is an annoying trait that can ruin even the best, funniest, perfectly structured speech, and that is a nervous speaker going too fast. This poor individual doesn't pause to let his points sink in, or even to receive the expected laughs. He just gallops on regardless, racing to the end as fast as possible. The guests spend all their time trying to keep up with this warp-speed commentary and don't even notice the jokes. Uh oh – no laughs. The unfortunate result of this is that the speaker, rather than slowing down and taking stock, panics and goes EVEN FASTER! And faster always spells disaster.

If you think you speak too fast in practice, good: at least you have noticed. And don't worry, even experienced speakers get this urge to speed up. The essential thing is not to give in to it. Plenty of practice and awareness of your breathing will help to slow you down. Start by trying to speak at half your normal speed. This will sound very slow to you, but better to start slow as you are bound to speed up once you get going. Try taking a drink at each pause (and writing PAUSE on your cue cards); it'll help you to leave more of a gap, as well as making you more refreshed. Always make sure you leave a pause after a funny, even when you're practising – then you'll do so automatically on the day. But remember that a pause is just that – a little bit of silence. Don't fill it with umms and ahs.

Stand tall and don't fidget!

When practising, remember, it's not all just words. People have to look at you as well as listen. Stand up straight and look confident – stand in front of a mirror if you need to, to make sure you don't start slouching partway through. Take particular care over this if you intend to read your speech; the tendency is to read down into the table, rather than out to the audience (see *Project yourself!* below). Look up at your audience whenever possible and make eye contact with people you are addressing by name. Smile – it will help you and your audience to relax and they'll be far more forgiving!

Fidgeting is usually the result of nerves, and can be very distracting for the audience. Unfortunately, the fidgeter often does not realise what he is doing. Hands in pockets invariably lead to jangling change or keys; hands out of pockets to hair-twiddling, jacket-straightening or tie-stroking, even nose-rubbing or nervous scratching. Avoid these by holding something (your notes or your glass) or using your hands to emphasise points in your speech. Don't rock, shuffle, sway or squirm while speaking: using a mirror or camcorder when rehearsing will help to pick up any instances of this. Don't be surprised if you do – most inexperienced speakers will move around a lot the first few times – just correct it. However, you must also avoid the opposite problem of standing in a frozen position – this looks almost as bad and will have your guests feeling as uncomfortable as you look. Break the tension by occasionally shifting your balance or turning slightly. But make it natural.

Project yourself!

Remember, this is a performance you are giving, not a bland recitation. When practising, make doubly sure that you pronounce all words clearly, and with correct emphasis. If you don't know how a word should sound (particularly difficult with some names), ask someone who knows, and practise it with them. Even newsreaders have to do this, so don't feel you should know. If it's not a name, and you still have difficulty with it, then find an alternative word – use a thesaurus if necessary.

Get the mood right

The way you pace your speech, and the amount and variety of emphasis you use, both verbal and through gestures, will really make a difference. It will give mood and personality to your words and help to distinguish the important from the flippant, the funny from the serious. Remember, a good speech-maker should get across his mood even to someone who can't hear his words – so, if you have the facility, try videoing yourself and playing it back with the sound turned down. Can others tell whether you are making a joke or toasting absent friends? Can you?

A word about microphones

Microphones have crept into wedding receptions in recent years. They never used to be needed. Are we producing a generation of weak-voiced bridegrooms, or is it just that we are so used to seeing microphones everywhere from the TV to the pulpit that we feel naked without one? They really aren't necessary at most receptions, if the room has good acoustics and is not overly large. Unless you have a guest list that exceeds 200, or includes a lot of noisy children, you can probably do without.

However, more and more people are using them, so here are a few tips for the mike-shy:

- You are not Noel Gallagher. Do not attempt to swallow or smooch the mike. Keep it a good four inches or more away from your mouth.

- Neither are you Elvis. Don't swing it around, hug it to your chest or hold it out like a lollipop.

- Don't breathe heavily, sneeze or cough directly into the mike.

- Don't shout – the whole purpose of a mike is to allow you to be heard when you speak at normal volume.

- If you get feedback (that awful screeching) when you first pick up the mike, don't worry. Someone should be responsible for sorting this out. Don't try to fix it yourself.

- Don't tap or scratch the mike to see if it is working.
- Don't switch it on until you are ready to start, and switch it off immediately afterwards.
- Keep it a good distance from any glasses, jugs and bottles, for safety reasons.

By now, it must be almost time for your performance!

Delivering your speech

So the big day has arrived. You have practised, and know how to project, animate and pace your speech. You have your cards ready and the hour approaches. You should be confident. So why are you a bag of nerves? Don't worry, just read the next few pages before you take the stage.

First, some things to remember:

- Your cards or notes
- A handkerchief – make it easily accessible!
- A glass of water
- Any cards or faxes you intend to read out
- Any visual aids – run through beforehand to check they're the right way up and in the right sequence
- Check your teeth for spinach!

Last-minute nerves

Calm down. Pour yourself a glass of water – no ice (it clinks – very distracting) and sip it slowly. Don't drink too much alcohol before speaking. You might think it helps, but your audience won't.

Before you start, while the previous speaker is finishing, practise some deep breathing (quietly!). Breathe in, hold for a count of eight. Out, count of eight. And so on. This will help to regulate your galloping heart and stop those beads of sweat from turning to rivers. When your turn arrives, refill your glass, stand slowly and take a few seconds to make sure you're comfortable (not squashed between chair and table, for example) and that if you're using a microphone it is at an appropriate height (don't tap it or blow in it – if it's not working, somebody will sort it out). When you are ready to start, look at the audience and establish eye contact first. Smile! Give a wink, if you like. Another deep breath, and then begin. Good luck!

Remember that there's no rush. Pause frequently, and take your time, sipping your water before launching back into it. Here are a few tips for handling particular problems.

Coughs, sneezes and hiccups

If you have to cough, sneeze or blow your nose, turn your head away from the microphone and guests to do so. If you have an uncontrollable coughing fit, indicate to the audience that you need to stop (hold up your hand, for example), switch off the mike, turn away and sip at your water until the cough subsides. Then return, clear your throat, apologise briefly, and continue. Don't make a big thing of it and don't rush to get back into it – it may take a little longer to ensure that tickle has finally gone, but better that than repeated stopping and starting.

Hiccups are another thing entirely as they are irritatingly difficult to get rid of. If you get a fit of the hiccups at an inopportune moment – like just before your speech – it is probably best to beg the guests' pardon and ask to make your speech a little later – easy if you are not the last speaker, but if you are, try to make sure you don't leave it too long or the opportunity (and all your preparation) will have been wasted.

Problems with your voice

If your voice starts to waver or speed up, concentrate on speaking clearly and slowly. Try to establish eye contact with your guests and smile. Relax, you'll be fine. If your voice starts to disappear, follow the advice given on coughing, clearing your throat (away from the mike) as necessary.

Perspiration

If you tend to perspire when nervous (or when under lights – some hotels seem deliberately to bake the top table under a spotlight on purpose) keep your handkerchief handy. Don't scrub or dab at your forehead; wipe it discreetly during a pause, replace the handkerchief and continue.

Muddled words
If you stumble over your words, don't panic. Mistakes happen, and the less you make of it, the less people will remember it. If it's a small mistake, just continue. If it's more noticeable, say 'pardon me, I mean…' or 'rather, that is…' or something to that effect. Don't apologise profusely – you'll draw attention to the mistake and the audience will lose the thread of your speech.

Laughs
If you expect a laugh – wait for it. If it doesn't come, make a further joke of it by telling people, in a mock-hurt voice, that they were supposed to laugh and refusing to go on until they do. That always works … unless the initial joke was truly awful! Don't begin again until the laughter has died down – enjoy it. If the laugh goes on too long, and the guests start talking among themselves, say 'Thank you' into the mike and continue.

Interruptions and noises
Most interruptions to your speech will be good-humoured – one advantage of a wedding speech over other public speaking engagements. So enjoy any interruptions, especially funny ones. Don't get upset that they are disturbing your flow. Interruptions provide time for thinking and breathing, and anyway, an extra bit of humour is always welcome.

Hecklers are not common at weddings, although there may be the odd drunken aside to contend with. It may be a 'friend' trying to unnerve you. It may be someone who's had too much to drink. It may be neither. If for some reason you do have a ranting guest, the best policy to adopt is to stay calm. This will endear you to the guests and make the heckler look even more stupid. Simply ignore the interruption – remember, this person is looking for a soapbox and your job is to deny him or her one. If the heckler persists, and no one acts to remove him, you may have to acknowledge and deal with him. Be polite and firm. Use humour if the situation warrants it (e.g. 'Somebody call the police – the village is missing its idiot!'), but be aware that getting a laugh, even at his own expense, may make the heckler more, rather than less, bold. If the person refuses to give in, it should be up to the venue staff to remove him.

Then there are the noises. Snoring is, unfortunately, rather common – and if it happens during your speech don't despair; it's far more likely to be caused by the wine than by your speech! If it's obvious to the rest of the guests, make a joke of it and this should prompt a swift elbow in the ribs from the snorer's companions. Other unwelcome noises include bawling children (who should of course always be taken out of the room); cheeky children (who can be used to great advantage, if you have the skills, otherwise a glare at the parents will usually suffice); passing ambulances, fire engines, police cavalcades, boy racers and even buses – all of which can be eased by a suitable joke. If the noise is too loud for you to be heard clearly, stop speaking until it is over, then make your joke, pause for laughs, then pick up where you left off. If the noise is less obtrusive, you can either pretend it isn't there or just make quick reference to it (in the case of the fire engine, for example: 'uh-oh, sounds like chef's used too much brandy in the flambé again') before continuing. The one exception, of course, is the fire alarm: if this goes off you must assume there is a fire, and unless someone else steps forward, as the current speaker you should urge calm and get everyone to leave in an orderly fashion by the nearest fire exit.

Last-minute announcements

We touched on this briefly in the preparation section. You may remember I suggested that some things can't be planned for: the sudden illness or even death of a guest; particularly disturbing news from the 'outside world'; a power cut; cancellation or delay to the catering or entertainment; evacuation of the venue; the list goes on. With these items, you are unlikely to get much notice, nor much instruction on what to say. But that's OK, nobody will expect it. Whatever the news, deliver it at the beginning of your speech (unless you are already speaking when it arrives, in which case as soon as possible), and then move on to your main speech, if appropriate.

Unless the 'news' or item particularly impinges on the wedding, it may be best not to mention it at all. How many of us, in the throes of our wedding celebrations, would really want to know if World War III had officially started? If it's not going to immediately affect the guests during the wedding, leave it out. If it's likely to ruin their day, definitely do so, unless you are instructed otherwise by the couple themselves. Of course, fire alarms and similar alerts should always be relayed to the guests, even if they turn out to be merely exercises.

A final word

If you're still nervous, remember…

- You're not going into combat: the guests are on your side. They are eagerly anticipating your speech, so give them the opportunity to enjoy themselves and it.

- If you get a totally unexpected laugh, check your flies – and the back of your cue cards!

- Five or ten minutes and it's all over, so is it really worth panicking about?

- When people are congratulating you afterwards, don't forget to mention this book!

Chapter 5
Dare to be Different

This chapter provides suggestions for how to make your speech truly memorable by adopting a different format or presentation style. It is probably most appropriate for the experienced speaker or presenter, although confident novice speakers may also find it useful. The styles discussed are most suitable for the best man's speech, but can also be used to great effect by other speakers, such as the chief bridesmaid, a family friend, or even the bride or groom.

Do you dare?

There are those among us for whom the thought of giving *any* kind of speech is daunting. (I'm one of them, which is why I write books instead.) To us, it makes no difference whether we are to stand up before a group of friends, an interview panel, a class of five-year-olds, or the national conference of the Women's Institute. Our knees knock, our throats dry up, we develop a curious wobble to our voices and a pronounced and previously unknown stutter. We sweat, we wring our hands, we faint. We forget half our words and get the other half in the wrong order. We really shouldn't be made to speak at all and we should definitely not attempt anything unusual. If this sounds like you, I suggest you concentrate on the tips for the nervous, in the previous chapter, and skip this chapter entirely. Unless, that is, your nerves stem purely from the audience *watching* you – in which case this section may provide the solution.

Of course, there are those for whom a speech containing only speech is not enough. Oh no. There needs to be more razzmatazz, more visuals, more laughs – just *more*. And this is great for the audience, so should be encouraged. As someone who's been on the receiving end of many a dull speech, I heartily applaud those who try to do something different and succeed. Their speeches stick in the mind where others dissolve. But attempting such a speech does take nerve, a certain amount of know-how, and a great deal of practice. If this sounds like you, read on.

When is it appropriate?

Generally, these visual or dramatic speeches work best at informal weddings with a fairly large audience – 60 or more – in a large room. However, many seriously pomp-laden weddings also feature such antics at the reception – which may be seen as an opportunity for relaxation after the ceremony. Several of the ideas given could also be adapted for the small, family-only affair. Whether or not such a speech is suitable for the wedding you are attending will generally depend on the following:

- Whether you, and the couple, are comfortable with the idea
- Whether you will have sufficient time on the day
- Whether suitable materials are available – e.g. photos, slides, video
- Whether the required equipment is available – e.g. a projector or video player and screen
- Whether the room is suitable – e.g. is it possible to block out light? Is there sufficient room for the equipment? Are power points placed suitably and safely? Will it be possible to walk among the guests?
- Whether you will have sufficient time to prepare the materials and practise, preferably at the venue, with the appropriate equipment.

If you can answer 'yes' to all the above, know your audience (see *Planning Your Speech*) and tailor your speech accordingly, there is no reason why this type of speech would not work for you.

Ideas for doing it differently

Here are a few of the more unusual approaches that I've experienced. They all work well, but you may have your own ideas.

The video diary

One for those who are *au fait* with the camcorder, this comprises a series of funny or embarrassing video clips of the victim – usually the groom but sometimes including the bride – often from an early age upwards, and often ends with a similarly embarrassing shot of the speech-maker, just to even things up. Of course, whether this will be possible depends a lot on the amount of footage available, for which you can selflessly blame the parents. Younger couples are more likely to have been filmed in their youth than older ones, although there may be the odd reel of cine film in the attic that will reap great rewards for the more senior bride and groom. These days many places will convert to VHS for you, and a black and white sequence of your bride or groom – ideally aged eight and sporting a saggy woollen swimsuit or particularly atrocious haircut – is just the thing.

Keep the video usage to short, amusing sequences that punctuate your speech, rather than replace it. If you prefer, and you have the technology to be able to do so, you could, however, completely replace your speech with a 'documentary style' video featuring you as narrator with contributions from friends plus the sequences previously described – great if you suffer from on-the-day nerves but are happy to speak to that little black box. Remember though that it will have to look professional to keep the interest, so if you've no experience of filming, don't attempt it.

The slide show

Along similar lines to the video diary, this is generally more practical as slides can be created from video or cine stills, camera prints or negatives, even particularly old ones and passport photos (which always raise a laugh). If you're particularly evil and have the skills, you can even create slides from made-up 'photos' using computer software.

Choose your slides carefully for maximum impact, and never forget how incredibly tedious it can be to sit through someone's holiday snaps – use a few key slides to accent particular points of your speech, not a continuous flow with short comments. If there's nothing funny about a slide, don't use it. Rather than a potted history of one person (usually the groom), try to include some of the bride's early years, to balance it out; a few choice snaps of the parents go down well too. When choosing slides, remember that some of the best expressions and funniest poses can often be found in the background of unrelated pictures. If you find one like this, it's worth taking the original to a photo lab to get the particular area you require cropped and enlarged, so it can appear on its own, rather than having to point out to your guests a small child in a larger photo of somebody else.

The Big Red Book approach

This owes something to the late Eamonn Andrews and his successors in *This Is Your Life*. It can be a lot of fun if done well.

Take one best man, one roving microphone and a roomful of

guests. Subject: *'The bride and* [especially] *groom. What can you tell us about them?'*

This also offers a great way to say very little yourself, and deflect all the embarrassment on to your audience. You will need to prime a few key people, to ensure you have some good anecdotes, but that's allowed – after all, most of the TV shows do the same! You will also need a good eye for someone with a story to tell, and the ability to avoid those who waffle or who would be too embarrassed to speak. One good way to ensure a wide selection of apt tales is to warn the guests beforehand. Select, say, half of the names on the guest list, then send each a short note asking them to rack their brains for something suitably short and amusing to tell about the happy couple. Or even about the parents – after all, why should they be allowed to escape?

Note that this one will only work in a room with enough space to roam about, and preferably one where the seating plan allows for everyone to see everyone else. You will also need a cordless microphone, or one with a long cord – if the latter, make sure any children will be seated at the time to avoid accidents. It's wise to also have someone on hand with a wristwatch, who will signal to you when your time is nearly up – otherwise this kind of speech can go on all night!

The theatrical approach

This may be considered rather a niche option; it's ideal for couples who are into amateur dramatics or theatre, but might not always work for everyone. The idea is to act out some of the anecdotes that you might otherwise have spoken about or shown on video. Usually involving a handful of close friends dressed in suitably daft costumes (including the obligatory outsized baby and the *Beano*-like schoolmaster), it requires some organisation, some willing participants, and some knowledge of dramatics. The format is up to you, but don't be too elaborate; it's really just a gimmick, not a professional stage play. If you've no experience of am-dram, don't bother with it – badly done it will not come across well.

The business presentation

This one is an ideal way to tease a groom (or even a bride) who is obsessed with his job, especially if that involves a team leader or management role. Use a flip chart, a projector, a laptop; whatever his favourite gadget is, and present your speech like a sales pitch. This will go down particularly well if the guests include several of his business colleagues, but you must remember that the idea here is humour – make it too serious and people will find it bizarre.

Using visual aids

Visual aids can include not just photographs and slides, but also video, sketches, computer graphics, picture images, even objects and models. They can be shown to the audience using equipment such as an overhead projector, slide projector or TV screen, or simply reproduced in a handout (which also doubles as a handy keepsake) to be given out at the appropriate time – hotel waiting staff will often hand them out when bringing coffee, if you ask them nicely. Try to time this with the start of your speech though; it's unfair on the other speakers if guests are flicking through this while they are trying to speak.

Remember, an effective visual aid supplements rather than replaces your speech. It should help to emphasise your points, with humour. Anything used as a visual aid should be relevant, simple, and clear (no fuzzy photos).

For those of you yet to be convinced, here are some tips on the benefits and use of visual aids.

* They enhance understanding of the topic
* They add authenticity, variety and (hopefully) humour
* They help your speech have lasting impact.

If you intend to use visual aids, keep in mind the following:

* Make sure the visual aid is integrated into your speech, so it doesn't jar

- Plan the placement of visual aids prior to the speech
- Practise cueing in the aids at the appropriate points, and run through the entire speech with aids in place at least once
- Check all equipment beforehand – make sure it is running, that you know how to operate it, and that any slides, etc. are in the right order and the right way up (it happens!)
- Do not display any equipment or images until you are ready to use them, then when you've finished, remove or cover the equipment.

Chapter 6
Ten Steps to the Perfect Wedding Speech

Here's a quick summary of what we've covered. Don't rely on just this page though, it's only to refresh your memory – read the details first!

1. Think ahead

Don't leave it to the last minute. Like the rest of the wedding, a speech should be given the planning and attention it deserves. Plan as far ahead as possible to avoid last-minute panics.

2. Know your audience

Get an impression of the 'average' guest, and from this choose subjects that everyone can relate to. Telling funny stories from the couple's past is a good idea, but not everyone finds the same things funny. Be sensitive to your audience, particularly older guests. Avoid anything that might be considered in bad taste, and keep the jokes and quotes simple and relevant.

3. Know your job

However unusual your wedding may be, there are things you must do in your role as speech-maker. Read the lists in *The Basics of Wedding Speeches* and make sure you include all the relevant thank-yous, toasts, and so on, in your speech, as well as the usual jokes and anecdotes.

4. Keep it short

Nobody likes a waffler. Time yourself when you first practise, and cut down ruthlessly until your speech is a maximum of eight minutes long, preferably five. The larger the wedding, and the more speakers there are, the shorter the speech need be. Remember, your main purpose is to toast, not to educate.

5. Write and rewrite

Don't just write your speech and put it away until the day. Instead, read it regularly, and each time you will probably find something you want to revise. A joke that previously sounded hilarious will somehow no longer fit, or a phrase will sound hackneyed. Don't be afraid to cut bits out, change the order or rewrite whole sections. Try not to rewrite the whole speech though, or you'll be back at square one.

6. Practise, practise, practise

Don't just rewrite – *practise*. Even before you have the final version, reading through your script will help you to memorise it, and to know when to pause, what expressions and gestures to use, which words you trip over, etc. Practise alone; out loud; in front of a mirror or camcorder; then in front of someone who will offer constructive criticism. Keep going until you are happy with your performance. If you're using a mike or other equipment, practise in the venue if at all possible.

7. Use notes

Even the most confident speaker occasionally loses his or her place. All it takes is an untimely interruption and you are left wondering what you were saying. To avoid this, always have notes to which you can refer – even if it's just one sheet of paper. Don't write out everything, just the key points, and use underlining or coloured pens to help draw your eye to the right place. Cue cards are ideal but make sure you number them and don't hold them up – try to use them discreetly.

8. Get ready

Do some deep breathing to relax you before your turn arrives. Pour yourself a glass of water and keep it handy but not somewhere that it might get knocked over. Go to the toilet before the speeches begin, and remember to check your teeth! Check the position of the mike, if you're using one, and discreetly check your notes before you stand up. Clear your throat before you start – but not while someone else is speaking.

9. Breathe and don't panic!

Take a deep breath at the beginning so that you don't run out of breath in the middle of a sentence. It's easy to say it, but try not to be overwhelmed by the situation: it's a happy occasion, you're not on trial. Everyone is here to enjoy themselves and is looking forward to your speech. If you make a mistake, just correct it and carry on. Try to relax – you'll appear much more confident.

10. Keep your audience interested

Watch your speed when practising, and on the day. Stand up straight and project your voice, without shouting (particularly if using a microphone). Look at the guests as you speak and use appropriate expressions. Pause noticeably after a joke or amusing anecdote, or where there is a change of emphasis (for example after a solemn toast). Introduce feeling in the way you speak and emphasise certain words both vocally and with gestures. Avoid rustling papers and notes, and keep your hands occupied to avoid distracting movements or habits. But most importantly – smile! Then your audience will smile with you.

Samples Library

This section gives a number of sample speeches that you can use to help you create your own unique speech, appropriate to the particular wedding you are attending. This is followed by a selection of suitable wedding toasts, and some apt quotations that you may like to drop into in your speech. For other examples see the books and web sites suggested in *Where to Find Out More* on page 149.

Speeches

Here you will find examples of speeches given at real weddings by all the usual speakers; some more unusual ones, given by, for example, the bride or bridesmaid, or by a substitute for one of the main speakers; and some written specifically for a second marriage.

Please do not use these speeches verbatim. They have been written with specific weddings and couples in mind, and will never be entirely suitable for yours. Instead, read several of them, plus the sections that follow, and use these to craft your own speech – taking sentences or ideas from these if you wish – using the methods described in this book.

Father of the bride

'Hello everybody. It's great to see you all on this wonderful day, both so many of our friends and family, and those of you whom we haven't met before. And all of us here enjoying ourselves, to see John marry my only daughter today. I am very happy to welcome John and all of his relatives into our family, and hope we will share many happy occasions in the future. I should also like to thank John's parents Terry and June for all their help with the wedding.

You know, standing up in front of all of you and making a speech about my only daughter and her new husband has got to have been one of the toughest assignments I have ever had to take on. Give me a projector and some lousy sales figures to present to a crowd of high-powered execs any day – you lot are far more frightening! [Pause for laughs]

When Jane was born I realised that I had a wonderful new gift in my life, and as the years have passed that gift has become dearer to me. Of course there have been ups and downs; she was a model teenager – it's just that, as any parent will tell you, the model for teenagers was faulty! There were times when I was the best dad in the world and then times when I just did not understand. But she has more than compensated for those times. Today is the most special day in her life and she deserves the most perfect of husbands. [Brief pause]

So, what about John? Well, if the guests here today are any indication of his worth, John should prove to be an excellent son-in-law. I should like to thank all of you on their behalf today for your generous gifts: they have been most gratefully received but, more importantly, you have given Jane and John the best start to their marriage, your best wishes.

Now I am sure John's parents think he is perfect ... but I have to be convinced. I've no doubt of his qualities as a husband, but as a son-in-law, will he in future learn to buy me a pint, or will I have to continue to buy his for him? [Enquiring glance at John]

Marriage can be a rocky road but love can make it smooth. I am sure that Jane, like her mother, my dear wife Angela, will have a warm and welcoming home at each stage of the journey. Certainly if she is as good a wife as Angie, John will have no complaints at all. I hope they are standing here in 25 years' time doing the same for their daughter as I am today – but a word of warning John: you'd better start saving now!

Today then I wish Jane and John a marriage filled with all the things that matter in life. I wish them trust and faith in each other. I wish them lots of laughter because laughter adds a shine to life. Above all though, I wish them the love that is a total commitment. With that and loyalty they can conquer the world.

Jane has enough love in her to make anything happen. So John, [Turn to groom] in having given you my darling Jane today, I know that you will share her with me. Cherish her and, speaking from experience, I know she will cherish you. [Turn back to audience]

Ladies and gentlemen, please raise your glasses in a toast to the bride and groom. [Pause to allow people to stand if required] To John and Jane ... may your love be modern enough to survive the modern times, and old fashioned enough to last forever.'

Or how about this one, slightly more formal, which can equally well be used by someone other than the father of the bride, if he is not present or not able to speak (see next page for further examples in this instance):

'Ladies and gentlemen: I have a very happy duty to perform today, on this happiest of occasions. I am going to ask you all to drink a toast to the health and happiness of our beautiful bride and her groom. It is an especially happy task because I can perform it with total confidence. They both look the picture of perfect health and their happiness is very obviously beyond concealment.

You know, marriage has sometimes been called a lottery, but I am sure there is no gamble about this match. Both Jane and John took a peek in advance at the winning numbers before they chose their tickets. Of course I could have told John that he had found a winner right from the start; because I've known Jane since she was a sweet and lovable child, and have watched her grow sweeter and more lovable with every year as she grew up. But John, wisely, did not ask my opinion, and neither did Jane. I hope they will both forgive me if I give it now, and say that, if ever a marriage was made in heaven, this is it. They met at the church, as many of you will already know; both members of the junior choir, their eyes met as their notes soared, and their hearts were joined in harmony. Today we saw them marry in the place they first met, and I am sure that harmony will continue throughout their lives.

No one ever forgets his wedding day, and this young couple will look back on this day with many a sweet memory as the years pass. I doubt if their memories will include my speech, so I shall detain you no longer.

Ladies and gentlemen, I ask you to drink to the health and happiness of the bride and groom.' [Pause to allow guests to stand, if required]

Substitutes for father of the bride

Some guidance on the use of substitutes is provided in the section *Traditional Speeches* on page 14.

If the bride's father is dead, the person making 'his' speech should refer to him tactfully, preferably near the beginning of the speech. For example:

'When I asked why I was chosen for this job, Jane said, "Well, you've known me since I was in nappies!" and that, I suppose, is as good a reason as any. Of course, this was partly because Jane's dear father Tom was my best friend. Jane and Angela particularly asked me not to leave him out of this speech, because although *he's no longer with us in person, we all still feel his loving presence, particularly on this wonderful day. For sure, he wouldn't want us to be sad on his account: had he been here, he would have told a good joke. So instead, I'll tell you one he told me some years ago. That way you can't blame me if it's awful!...'*

Reference can similarly be made to other recently departed family members – but don't turn it into a long list. For example:

'Of course, there are people who aren't with us today, who are greatly missed. Emily's dear father Gordon should, of course, have been making this speech today. How proud he would have been to see his daughter looking so radiant and happy, after the strain of his last months. Emily, and all her family, are a great credit to him today and we are sure he is watching over us in great joy on her special day. Also Nanna Jean, who passed away last year, would have loved to be here today, as would John's grandparents Grace and Henry, who are also sadly no longer with us. We are thinking of them all today.' [Brief pause before continuing]

The rest of the speech can then continue as usual, without further reference to the subject. Occasionally a toast is made, but if so, it is usual to include this as a more general toast to absent friends to avoid making the atmosphere too morbid.

Sometimes, the bride's mother may like to say a few words on her late husband's behalf. This is usually a short speech of its own rather than a replacement for the 'father of the bride' speech, which may still be performed by someone else. For example:

'Ladies and gentlemen: I just wanted to say a few words on behalf of Tom and his family. The last few months have been hard for all of us, and it's a great relief to be able to dispel all that with this wonderful occasion. It's like a new beginning, not just for Jane and John, but for the rest of us as well – their happiness has washed our sadness away. Tom was so looking forward to this day, and my only regret is that he was not here to see it, but I'm sure he is looking down at us now and smiling. Perhaps we can help him to be with us in two ways: first by a quiet moment to remember all the happy times, and then by continuing with this reception just as he would have wished. [Pause, head bowed, for a few seconds]*

This world is a better place for Tom having been with us. Without him, my life would have been empty and our beautiful daughters would never have been born. There would be no wedding today. All of our lives were enriched by his happy-go-lucky nature and his ready wit.

And now, as he'd put it, let's get on with it, girl!'

Of course, the bride's father may not be dead – he may merely be unable to speak, either through illness or absence. If absent, the circumstances will dictate whether his name should be mentioned; if ill, a wish for his speedy recovery (if that is feasible) will suffice.

Bridegroom

This one should be short, light-hearted and full of praise for both bride and bridesmaids (if any), as well as fulsome thanks to both sets of parents. Remember, you will be nervous enough on the day, even if the main event is finished, so don't try for any fancy styles or a longwinded speech. Here's a particularly good short speech that covers all you need to say; just tailor it to include your personal 'extras':

'Ladies and gentlemen: My wife and I – I must get used to calling her that, it still seems rather strange – anyway, my wife and I thank you all most sincerely for your kind wishes. I am sure you will excuse me from making a long speech, and will understand that, at the moment I am quite incapable of making one. I don't need to tell you that I think I am the luckiest man in the world, and that my only ambition is to be worthy of my luck – that is, of Jane. I must add that today I have not only gained the best wife that any man could hope for, but I have also acquired an extra mother and father in Tom and Angela. [Indicate bride's parents] No parents could have been kinder and more helpful to

a man bent on stealing away their daughter. Other than my own, of course, [Indicate own parents] who are probably as keen for her to take me so they can redecorate my room!

Before I sit down, I must ask you to join me in drinking to the health of these very charming and pretty ladies [Indicate bridesmaids] who have supported my wife in her ... I was going to say 'ordeal', but I think it's hardly been that ... her starring role, today. They deserve the best of praise and thanks for making sure she got here, and for keeping your eyes off my wife by looking so elegant themselves.

Ladies and gentlemen – the bridesmaids!'

Or:

'Hello everyone. Thank you all for being here on our big day.

You know, I told my new father-in-law a few minutes ago that I felt nervous about making this speech. He said, "Don't be silly. Everyone expects a man to make a fool of himself on his wedding day. They'll be disappointed if you don't!" And the last thing I want to do is disappoint you! I feel so happy that I want everyone else to be as happy too.

Let me say too, how delighted Jane and I are that you were all able to come to our wedding, despite the last-minute change of arrangements when Jane was taken ill last month. Thank you all so much for bearing with us and for all your good wishes for Jane's recovery. As you can see, she's looking more than recovered today, and I'm very glad you're all here to appreciate it. Quite apart from anything else, we'd have felt very foolish sitting down here behind this enormous cake if there was no one here to eat it! And the photos would have been a bit empty too! But we do sincerely thank you all for coming, and for the beautiful presents you have so generously given us, and hope to welcome you all to our new home in the near future – but not all at once please!

Now I'm not going to take up much of your time. But I do have a few personal thank-yous to make. Firstly, I must thank Jane's parents, Bob and Angie, for this marvellous reception. Now they are my 'in-laws', a phrase that suggests all sorts of jokes. But I don't like that phrase much, so I hope they don't mind me calling them my "extra" mum and dad, because that's what they've been like these past few years, and I hope will continue to be. I will certainly do my best to be a good son-in-law to them. Then, of course, there's my own parents, who have done so much for me throughout the years, who have guided and helped me through all sorts of difficulties and who have helped us to get our new home ready. And of course, I must thank my best man. You wouldn't think, to see him sitting here knocking back the champagne, that he's been particularly useful. But he has – without him I would probably still have been rummaging around at home for my bow tie. Not to mention the ring. He's a great organiser, and I must make a note to book him for the next time we have a big party.

Lastly, and by no means least, there are the bridesmaids and our young pageboy. One of my "official" duties in this speech is to thank them, but I would have done so anyway. The girls have helped Jane immensely, not only today, but throughout the long weeks of preparation, and both they and young Jamie have carried out their duties handsomely – and how wonderful they all look! We have a little gift for each of them as a token of our appreciation, but meanwhile would you please all raise your glasses in a toast to – the bridesmaids and pageboy.'

Best man

Remember, this is intended to be funny. Here are some great examples.

In the first example, there were no bridesmaids, so there is no toast to reply to. (This is more common than you might think). In this case, the speech was supported by slides. Note how just a few are used, to great effect, to avoid it becoming predictable.

'Well now everyone, let me introduce myself while I still can. My name is Stuart – I'm John's brother and I'd like to say a few words as his best man.

I'll try to keep this short. [Remove a thick block of cue cards from jacket pocket and expect a laugh] *Don't be fooled by these* [Indicate cards]. *You see, while planning this speech, John – or rather Jane – gave me a list of topics that I shouldn't cover*

[Remove all but a few cards], *so there goes most of the speech.*
But don't worry. I still have plenty of interesting stories. When
you've known John for as long as I have, you're never short on
material. [Knowing wink at audience]

Those of us who have known John throughout the years will
agree that he's a man who really knows how to experience life.
He takes advantage of his many talents to really grab all that life
has to offer. And you can imagine, as his younger brother, I've
learned a great deal from him – I usually do the opposite of what
he's doing – it's served me well.

John has gone through many evolutionary changes to end up
the man he is today. Before we begin to analyse exactly what
went wrong, let's examine his many career goals.

As many of you know, John has been climbing the ladder in
advertising in recent years. This comes as no surprise since he has
always been able to talk his way out of anything. You know, our
parents still believe that it really wasn't him who set the kitchen
on fire … John's talent for being able to spin any disaster into
an insurance claim developed early in life.

When Johnny was about to flunk school, he wanted to gain
his independence so he left home and got a job to support
himself. He told everyone he was working as a chef. It turns out
he was flipping burgers at McDonald's. Later when he went to
college I remember how proudly he told everyone about his
grades one term: "I got only one 'C' and an 'A' in everything
else." He was only taking two classes.

Then there was a time when John wanted to become a rock star. My ears are still ringing, so we won't ask him to perform, but, just to keep you all awake, I've taken the liberty of preparing some visual aids to remind you of this particular phase. [Point towards projector, load slide one]

Here we go: this is him on stage one night. Yep, that's right. That's him under all that hair and make-up. I think his lipstick is on crooked but that's OK, he was just starting out. Now he always gets it perfect first time.

John always enjoyed being the centre of attention so he would often throw parties inviting all of his friends and the band – oh, sorry Mum and Dad, let the cat out of the bag there, did I? I bet you were wondering where that cherry brandy had gone … terrible stuff … Anyhow, here is another picture of your darling son, hosting one of those parties. [Load slide two and pause]

When the lure of the groupies and life on the road got to be a little much for John, he decided he wanted to become a businessman. So he started his own recruitment company, which was actually quite successful. So he thought that it was time to make some changes in his life so that he would be taken a little more seriously. [Load slide three] *Here he is conducting business on the phone. You'll notice he still has the long hair and earrings but he is wearing a nice suit. He thought that the suit would make him look a little more respectable … I think he was expecting too much from the suit.*

Anyway, he did have an extremely lucrative run with this business but before long John got bored and decided that he was wasting his talents.

With his quick wit, silver tongue and the great talent of thinking on his feet, it had to be either advertising or politics. We had a narrow escape, folks. Anyway, taking one more step on the ladder of evolution, John finally got his hair cut and he is still wearing a nice suit. No doubt that'll all change now he's married!

So as you can see and as I'm sure Jane has already discovered, John is a man of amazing talents. But perhaps his best talent was in finding the right mate.

John, you married Jane today and she is smart, beautiful, loving and caring, and she really deserves a good husband – it's just as well you married her before she found one!

But on a serious note. Johnny and I have had some excellent times together. He has been a great brother to me over the years, and if that's any indication of the kind of husband he'll be, Jane is a very lucky girl. And if it's not, I'm sure she'll make sure he toes the line!

Jane, please put your left hand on the table. Johnny, please put your hand on top of Jane's. Ladies and gentlemen, I want all of you to witness the last time John has the upper hand.

And now, it gives me great pleasure to invite you all to raise your glasses in a toast to John and Jane, the new Mr and Mrs Jones.

Here's to a long, healthy, and happy marriage. Cheers.'

Or this one, a good, all-purpose funny speech that you can easily adapt:

'Ladies and gentlemen, friends and – others. Well, they told me to include everybody!

It is my great pleasure to be here with you on this occasion to help Jane and John celebrate their marriage. However, to be best man is a special honour, and I particularly thank Jane and John for that. I know they really wanted someone rich and famous, so I'll pass the hat round afterwards and you make sure to tell everyone about me!

My first job is to reply to the toast you made to our wonderful bridesmaids and pageboy. We obviously all agree how marvellous they've been and I thank him on their behalf for his gifts.

I am sure you would also want me to give the happy couple the traditional best man's wish: may all their troubles be little ones, all their hopes big ones, and their happiness unending.

You will expect me to have a bit of fun at John's expense, but John's expenses have been so high recently that I think we'll have to pass his hat round too!

Seriously, one of the best man's duties is to sing the groom's praises and tell everyone about John's good points. The problem is, one, I can't sing, and two, he hasn't got any good points – apart from the obvious ones, that is, of being generous, kind-hearted, good-natured, handsome and modest – just like me!

Actually, John's a lot more modest than I am, but then perhaps he's got more to be modest about!

Some of you may wonder how a nice girl like Jane came to marry John. When John was younger he wasn't much of a hit with the girls. So he changed his aftershave and bought some new Y-fronts. Nothing happened. He bought all the copies he could find of Cosmo, and read them all. The girls just giggled. He did a crash course in personal magnetism. Zero. Zilch. Then he met Jane, the only woman in the world for him. And to his, and our, great amazement, she'd have him!

All he had to do then was resign from his honoured position as a bachelor. And there couldn't be a better reason for resigning than getting married to the lovely Jane. He's a very lucky fella!

So, thanks to Jane and John's marriage today, we have been privileged to come here and enjoy the celebrations with them. I would now like to offer warm and sincere thanks once more, to all those who have helped to make this such a successful, happy and memorable occasion. Thank you all very much. And now, of course, a toast to the bride and groom.'

Or how about this one, which is very short and to the point. It is intended for use at a wedding with older bridesmaids, not children. It could easily be adapted to be the first part of a longer speech, as it sets the tone well.

'Ladies and gentlemen: I am sure that the bridesmaids are very grateful for the kind things you have said about them. While it is my duty, as best man, to respond upon their behalf – although I'm quite sure they could adequately respond for themselves! – I cannot take it upon myself to voice their thoughts, because I am sure they are not the same as my own. When I am not thinking about our beautiful bride – and let's be honest, it's difficult to stop thinking about her! – I find my thoughts go automatically to the beautiful bridesmaids. As a matter of fact, although I confess to not knowing a lot about the origin of traditional wedding customs, I imagine that one of their main functions is to distract the best man's attention away from the bride. For while my admiration for Jane must be tempered by proper respect for John – or I would really be in trouble! – there is happily no such restraint on my feelings towards these wonderful bridesmaids, and – well, I'd better stop there before I give away too much, for, unlike John, I am of course still a bachelor!'

Best woman/bridesmaid

A speech of this type is becoming more common, especially among younger couples. It should be light in tone, similar to the best man, but less risqué if the audience includes older people. If all the guests are twenty-somethings, that's different – be as rude as you like!

Here are a couple of examples.

'Ladies and gentlemen: you'll be pleased to know I am only going to speak for a couple of minutes ... you know, bridesmaids are traditionally not supposed to speak at all, but I had to squeeze in a few words.

I first got to know Jane and John during that most awkward stage of life, the teenage years. Like most of us, they both did many embarrassing things that they never told their parents about. I've brought a list of all of them here tonight. [Bring out very long list.] Just kidding – my mum's here too, you know!

My first memories of our happy couple may surprise you, although I'm sure you'll see some similarities still. Let's look at Jane first.

Jane was the loudest of all of my schoolfriends, without a doubt. She had a terrible hairdo and endless spots, used some dreadful language, and knew all the lyrics to every pop song. Her favourite way of annoying me was to claim that The Spice Girls were better than Boyzone. Sorry Janie, but we were BOTH wrong – these days it just HAS to be Westlife!

Johnny was a lot quieter than Jane, but he also managed to stick out like a sore thumb: he was the only swimmer in the school team with long hair. Everyone else had a number two, which was quite useful: you could always tell which one was Johnny even from the other end of the pool! When he first left school he instantly became everyone's best friend because of his job at McDonald's – he narrowly escaped the sack after giving us all free shakes and fries one Saturday in front of his boss. Of *course, he talked his way out of it as he always does! He wasn't very happy there anyway because they made him wear his hair in a net and he thought that was a bit girlie!*

Jane and John have always been a good team. When we all went out clubbing and had a few drinks, Johnny could be relied upon to be the responsible one and drag all of us safely home. At this time he drove a clapped-out Mini that was meant to carry only four passengers at a squeeze but more often held seven – not exactly the magnificent seven, all right, particularly after a night out, but being the only one of us with a car, he had no choice. In return, when Johnny made a particularly unfunny joke, Jane would laugh for everyone else, and, though she'll probably kill you for telling me this, she always ironed his McDonald's uniform!

But, as fun as it is to assassinate their characters, I must admit that John and Jane's relationship is more than just nights out and bad jokes. They have grown from school sweethearts into mature adults who understand that a relationship requires commitment and compromise. Their love and trust has endured through thick and thin; a quality that will no doubt come in handy in the years to come.

Now it gives me immense pleasure – and relief – to invite you all to raise your glasses in a toast to my best friends – John and Jane.'

Or this one:

'Ladies and gentlemen: Well, what can I say? What a wonderful meal, and beautifully served, to complement such a perfect day. Let's all raise our glasses to the chef. [Brief toast]

Now, as most of you will know, Jane is my big sister and, because we have always been close, she begged me to make a speech. In fact she made it a condition of my being her bridesmaid. She knew I couldn't resist this dress, so I had no choice! But I'm very nervous, so please bear with me.

With Dad being posted abroad when we were young, and Mum having Gran to look after for many years, Janie and I spent a lot of our childhood on our own. Now don't think I'm complaining, I think being left to do your own thing at that age is just what every child wants – our friends used to envy us our freedom and the way we always invented games to play and things to do. But that was always down to Jane, really, she's always been the resourceful one. She'd have me making things and crawling into things all day once she had some plan in her head. And I loved it! She taught me a lot about life as, being older, she went through everything before me. She told me what school was like, and taught me how to climb drainpipes when I wanted to get out at night ... oops, sorry mum! ... and she always helped me with my homework. Even when she left home she would come over and make sure I was doing all right. When Hayley was born, she asked me to be godmother, and that was the proudest day of my life ... until today. Now Hayley officially has the daddy she loves, and Jane the husband she adores. Dad is no longer with us, of course, but Mum and I are so proud today, and so pleased to welcome William into our little family. And his family have been so wonderful to us, not just kind and helpful, but loving – they have become our best friends. Thank you all.

Now what advice can I offer you, Jane and Bill, on your wedding day? Well, since you've always been the one dishing out the advice, Jane, it'll have to be something you once said to me. "Never go to bed mad. Stay up and fight. Then go to bed and make up." Thank you.'

Bride

Speeches by the bride are a fairly recent innovation, so you will find few samples in older books on which to base your speech. Here are a couple. Generally a bride's speech should follow a similar style to her groom's, praising parents and new spouse, thanking bridesmaids and friends, and the odd joke or quote about marriage. Although the first of these speeches is of similar length to the others in this book, as it in fact replaced the groom's speech at this wedding, in general the bride's speech is kept short. By the time she speaks the guests will probably have already heard several speeches and be getting restless.

'Well, as this is rather a non-traditional wedding, I thought it only appropriate that the bride should speak! It's always hard to keep me quiet and today is no exception.

I feel privileged to be sharing our special day with so many of the friends and family who are important to us. Some of our guests have travelled an awfully long way [Name some of the furthest places] to be here today, so thank you all for the effort you have made to get here. Many of you have had to take time off work too, so we thank you for that, and hope you have enjoyed it more than another day at the office!

You know, John and I have been together over seven years now, and during that time we've been through a lot. What can I say about John after all that time? Well, for a start, he has so many wonderful qualities … [Pause] charm, brains, beauty – are sadly the only ones missing!

But seriously, I would like to thank John for being the person that he is. He is not jealous, nor insecure, nor proud. He is welcoming to my friends, and is good company. He is funny, affectionate and loving. He is laid back and generous, and well worth all the effort I've put in! And it means a lot to be John's wife after seven long years of being his girlfriend.

A lot of people seem to think there is a big difference to your relationship once you get married. Someone told me that before marriage a man will lie awake all night thinking about something you said; after marriage he'll fall asleep before you have finished saying it. I don't need to worry about that one –

I'll just write it on the mirror: he spends so much time looking at himself, he'll never miss it!

I know that our opinion of marriage today is a lot more positive, I hope that in 20 years' time we will still have the same opinion – I'll keep you posted.

The main reason I wanted to speak today was to personally say thank you to some very special people who have contributed to this, our big day. First, of course, are my parents, who have been wonderful. They insisted on the best of everything, and refused to let me cut corners, as I'm sure you can tell.

I would also like to thank my sister Alice for being my bridesmaid: thanks sis, you've been great. And all you guys, go clean up before you ask her to dance, she's very particular about her dress. And why not, she looks better than me.

The next people I would like to thank are two of my best friends. Janet and Liz have always been there for me over the years when I really needed them, and girls, this thank-you is not just for the help you've given me for today, but for the friendship you've shown me over the years. I only hope I've been as good a friend to you. It was Janet who helped me choose the flowers, and she would be sitting up here today as matron of honour had Paul not gone and got her pregnant eight months ago – she refused point blank after that! Liz, of course, made the beautiful wedding cake that you see here before me – Lizzie I love you. Thank you so much for your help, you really are amazing.

Well, that's it but for one final thought. As we're on the subject of cake, here's some advice for all you ladies: if you think the way to a man's heart is through his stomach you're aiming too high.'

Or this, which is shorter yet still covers everything:

'Friends, family, all of you, everybody has told me not to make a speech today. You'll only cry into the wedding cake, they said. But you know me, I like a challenge! And I probably will cry all right, but they'll be tears of happiness and Simon has a large hanky ready. See what a considerate husband I have!

Anyway, I am not going to speak for long, but I just wanted to thank you all myself for coming to our special day, for sharing it with us. And of course to my parents for their love and patience with me over the years ... and Lord, did I try that patience! Sorry Mum and Dad. I'll try to behave from now on. I'm sure Simon will keep me in line!

Now it may be some while before we all meet up again, as Susie [bride's sister] shows no inclination to get married yet ... well she's a few years left before she's on the shelf, I suppose ... anyway, as we may not see each other for a while, I'd like to propose a final toast for the day, if I may. There's no need for you to stand and raise your glasses, for this is my toast to you. [Pause] To my wonderful husband and both our loving families; to all our friends old and new; I drink to your good health and happiness always.' [Bride drinks the toast alone]

Mother or father of the groom

The groom's parents often feel rather left out at the wedding reception. While the bride's father is expected to make a speech full of praise for his daughter and her new husband, they sit alongside and don't get their say. Well that's all changing! These days, many a father or mother of the groom stands to say a few words – or more – about their son and to welcome his new wife to the family. Here are a few examples. In the first, the newlyweds are about to move some distance away, so reference is made to this within the speech. (This, of course, could be adapted to fit in any speech, not just the groom's parents'.)

'Ladies and gentlemen, before we allow Stuart the floor to tell us all the embarrassing things he's found out about John, I'd like to have a few words: it's OK, John, I promise it'll only be a very few. I know it's not 'traditional' for the groom's parents to give a speech, but then this wedding hasn't been very traditional either, and we've all enjoyed it so far, haven't we?

Our bride and groom certainly have. And so they should – they deserve the very best. They have taken their time in getting around to it; not that any of us doubted they ever would, but I'm sure we're all pleased that they finally made it, and can now start their new life together as man and wife, as well as mummy and daddy to Emily, and of course as Doctor and Mrs Chapman in their new practice in Bromley. So many changes!

But, John and Jane, although you're embarking on a new and exciting episode in your life, and will be living so far away, Jean and I would like you to remember that we will always be here for you both whenever you need us, and even when you don't. Jane, you have always been a big part of our family since you first turned up with John all those years ago, and we hope you already consider yourself as much our daughter as you are John's wife. We already know you and John make a wonderful team, and your love for your daughter shines out like a beacon. John, you have done us proud over the years, both as a son and in your studies: we hope you will continue to do well with Jane's love and support and we congratulate you again on becoming the latest in a long line of Doctors Chapman. And of course we mustn't forget our darling little Emily, who has been so excited for her mummy and daddy all day and has been the perfect flower girl, I'm sure you will all agree. Jean and I will miss her terribly, of course, but it's been wonderful to see this little family grow and now we must set them free on their new path. We love you all dearly and wish you the best of good fortune.

Ladies and gentlemen, would you join me in a toast. John and Jane:

May your troubles be less
And your blessings be more.
And nothing but happiness
Come through your door.
Thank you.'

Now here is another, this time by the mother of the groom.

'Dear friends, it is rather unusual, I realise, for women to speak at a wedding, especially when they are the groom's mother, who is usually relegated to smiling sweetly and sipping quietly. Of course many of you who know me realise I wouldn't pass up the opportunity to have my say! But I promise to be brief.

First, a warning to you, Jane. If you ever have children, watch out! Tom was so accident-prone as a child that he almost got his own bed set aside for him in Casualty! If there was a hole for him to get wedged in, a ledge for him to fall off, or something to get stuck in his ears, nose or other, more unmentionable places, he'd find it without fail. His medical notes read like a dictionary of household dangers and he seemed to actively seek out new hazards to present at A&E. He had his favourites, of course. Baked beans up the nose was one. Getting his head stuck in the dog kennel. Falling off the pile of boxes he'd build to reach the biscuit tin. When he was three or four, we used to joke that he fancied the nurses, but he took such a long time to grow out of this that we actually started to wonder whether we were right! I mean, what other 14-year old manages to staple his big toe, scald his arm with a Pot Noodle and set fire to his hair all in one week?

Thankfully, he seems to have grown out of most of it since his teenage years, and now, of course, he has his own nurse in Jane, so he doesn't have to resort to the baked beans any longer. So you shouldn't have too much trouble with him. I know you'll take good care of him whatever scrapes he manages to get into, and I know he will do the same for you. You can count yourselves blessed to have found each other, and in each other such a wonderful love, respect and desire to achieve happiness as a family. I, and all of our family, wish you both the very best for the future.

And now, before I finally let Joe have the floor, ladies and gentlemen, please join me in a toast to our happy, injury-free couple. To Tom and Jane – the bride and groom.'

Speeches for a second marriage

Speeches for a second marriage are generally different in tone, and somewhat shorter than for a first. Some guidance is given in the section *Second marriages and late marriages* on page 25. Here are a couple of examples; the first by a friend, proposing the couple's health and happiness; the second the response from the groom.

'Dear friends: It's my great pleasure today to propose the health of our "happy couple", Deirdre and Bob, on this, their long-awaited wedding day. All marriages are special, and second marriages are doubly so – they are a time for renewed hope.

I'm sure all of us were delighted when Deirdre and Bob finally named the day. We all knew how perfect they were for each other, before they'd even realised it for themselves. You know,

Bob's brother Simon and myself spent weeks in the pub discussing how best to get them together. In the end we didn't have to: once they'd both stopped being so busy sorting things out for everyone else and put themselves first for a change, they found each other and that was that. Well, not exactly, I mean, it's taken them five years to get to this point, but no one can blame them for a bit of caution – after all, I'm sure they enjoyed those five years anyway!

Bob told me as we were getting ready this morning how grateful he was for this second chance at happiness. But as I pointed out to him, it's beyond a chance – in Deirdre he's already got the happiness he deserves, and so has she. Today is just about proving that to the rest of the world. And I'm sure the rest of the world, or everyone here today, at least, will join me in wishing you both the very best of happiness and a wonderful future together.

Let us raise our glasses then, to the bride and groom. Ladies and gentlemen – to Deirdre and Bob.'

The response by the groom should be equally brief:

'Thank you, Colin, for your kind words. Now everybody, Deirdre and I are so pleased to have you all here with us today. It's been such a wonderful occasion, made more so by the chance to see all your smiling faces and to know that we have such good friends.

You know, I never thought I'd see this day. After Judith died, I spent so many years shutting myself away, hiding in my work to try and block out the sadness. I never thought I'd be so happy again. But Deirdre has brought me all that, and for that, and all her other wonderful gifts, I am truly grateful. And now she is my wife and we have a new life to look forward to.

And part of that life will always be with our children, both Deirdre's son Alan and my own daughters Jenny and Rose, and all of their families. They have all been so supportive and helpful with the wedding arrangements – I couldn't believe how much arranging was needed for such a small wedding! – and have encouraged our friendship, and now our marriage, from the very start. We are so fortunate to have such a loving family around us.

Long may it continue. And may all of you here, family and friends alike, share many a happy occasion with this new family in the future. Thank you all.'

Bride's or groom's son or daughter

With the increase in remarriages, it is no longer uncommon for a child of one or both of the couple to make a speech. Normally, of course, this only occurs when the child is already an adult – or in his or her teenage years, at least. Sometimes, however, younger children can say a few words, and if both the bride and her groom have one or more 'pre-existing' children, they may choose to deliver a speech, or even a song, poem or story, together. This helps them to feel they are more a part of the wedding, and helps with getting them used to organising things together as part of the same family.

For example, at a recent wedding the groom's eight-year-old daughter and the bride's ten-year-old daughter performed a rendition of a well-known pop song about love and said how happy they were to be becoming sisters. At another the bride's 24-year-old son (who also gave her away) said a few lines, and was followed by his sister, who gave a longer speech. Both welcomed the new groom into the family and thanked him for his help and support over recent years. Here is the gist of the daughter's speech.

'Ladies and gentlemen. Mum says that I never shut up, and she's right. I certainly can't shut up about how happy I am to be here today, seeing her and David finally tie the knot. As you know, both Kevin [Bride's son] and myself have got married in recent years, and we both highly recommend it. We both worried when we left home that Mum would hate to be on her own with nobody to mother. But when she finally met David three years ago, we knew it was all right. They just clicked together and that was that. He is the man she has been looking for all these years: and nobody deserves it more than she does.

Kevin and I were too young when Dad died to remember much about it, especially as he'd been based abroad for all but Christmas and holidays. Yet Mum, who had known him since she was five, had lost the love of her life and there she was, miles away from her family in a new place where she knew nobody. It would have been so easy for her to fall apart: I'm sure many of us would have, in the circumstances. But Mum picked herself up and started to make a new home for the three of us. And for the next 15 years that's what she did. We wanted for nothing. She worked long and hard and fought for us on every front. It wasn't easy for her, and she never complained. Friends came and went, and boyfriends, but they never lasted because they couldn't compete with Kevin and myself – and we made their lives hell! But we knew none of them were ever right, and I'm sure Mum did too. She just wasn't interested: she used to say her only aim was to get us through school and see us settled, and then she'd worry about herself. And she did get us through school, and Kevin through college. And just when we were all wondering what next, along came David and changed everything. We knew he was the right one – Mum got her hair cut. She started wearing perfume and dressing up. It was great to see that for once Mum really was thinking of herself. And David never tried to come between us. When he'd been seeing Mum for a few weeks he sat down with Kevin and me and told us how much he liked her, and asked what he could do to make us all happy. We interrogated him for an hour! But although the subject of marriage never came up on that occasion, neither of us was surprised when, a few weeks later, David took us aside again and suggested it. He was heartbroken when Mum turned him down. But finally she's seen sense and now she's no longer just our mum, but David's wife as well. And she looks wonderful on it. David, thank you so much for bringing our mother so much joy. You have made all our lives complete.

So now, ladies and gents, please all join me in toasting the happy couple …'

Often with second marriages the child of one or other party may be best man or bridesmaid, so read the sample speeches in those sections too for further ideas.

Toasts

Most of these toasts are suitable for general use, but there are also some additional sections to cover particular scenarios or audiences.

Toasts to the couple

As [Groom] *and* [Bride] *start their new life,*
Let's toast the new husband and wife!

May there always be work for your hands to do.
May your purse always hold a coin or two.
May the sun always shine warm on your windowpane.
May a rainbow be certain to follow each rain.
May the hand of a friend always be near you
And may you fill each other's hearts with joy to cheer you.

May your lives be long and happy,
Your cares and sorrows few;
And the many friends around you
Prove faithful, fond and true.
May you grow old on one pillow.

May you see each other through many dark days, and make all the rest a little brighter.

May you look back fifty years from now and agree that today was the worst day of your married life.

To the bride and groom – may we all be invited to your golden wedding celebrations.

Live life to the fullest – remember, this is the first day of the rest of your life.

May you get all your wishes but one, so you always have something to strive for!

May all your joys be pure joys,
And all your pain champagne.

To the newlyweds: May 'for better or worse' be far better than worse.

May you taste the sweetest pleasures that fortune ere bestowed,
And may all your friends remember all the favours you are owed.

To all the days from here and after
May they be filled with fond memories, happiness and laughter.

Happiness being a dessert so sweet
May life give you more than you can ever eat.

May your laugh, your love and your wine be plenty,
Your happiness endure and your life be never empty.

May your home always be too small to hold all your friends.

I wish you health, I wish you wealth and happiness galore.
I wish you luck in all you do; what could I wish you more?

May your joys be as deep as the oceans, your troubles as light as its foam.
And may you find sweet peace of mind, wherever you may roam.

May your right hand always be stretched out in friendship and never in want.

May you both live as long as you want,
And never want as long as you live.

May your glass be ever full.
May the roof over your heads be always strong.
And may you be in heaven half an hour
Before the devil knows you're dead.

May you be poor in misfortune,
Rich in blessings,
Slow to make enemies,
And quick to make friends.

May the most you wish for be the least you get.

May your troubles be less
And your blessings be more.
And nothing but happiness
Come through your door.
Whether rich or poor, quick or slow,
May you know nothing but happiness
From this day forward.

May the saddest day of your future be no worse than the
happiest day of your past.

Here's to the bride and the bridegroom,
We'll ask their success in our prayers,
And through life's dark shadows and sunshine
That good luck may always be theirs.

May the roof above us never fall in.
And may the friends gathered below it never fall out.

The following is ideal as a toast by a parent of bride or groom:

It is written: when children find true love, parents find true joy.
Here's to your joy and ours, from this day forward.

The following are amusing, but may be unsuitable for particularly formal weddings.

As you slide down the banister of life,
May the splinters never point the wrong way.

As you ramble through life, whatever be your goal;
Keep your eye upon the doughnut, and not upon the hole.

May the winds of fortune sail you,
May you sail a gentle sea.
May it always be the other guy
Who says, 'This drink's on me.'

Here's to the bride that was married today,
Here's to the groom she wed,
May all their troubles be light as bubbles
Or the feathers that make up their bed!
To keep a marriage brimming
With love in the loving cup,
When you are wrong, admit it,
And when you are right, shut up!

Here's to you both, a beautiful pair,
On the birthday of your love affair.

Here's to the husband
And here's to the wife.
May they be lovers
The rest of their life.

Religious toasts
Only use these where there is no religious difference between
the couple or their families.

May God bless you both and keep your hearts as one.

May these rich blessings be your due,
A wealth of friendships, old and new,
Quiet nights and busy days,
Time for prayer and time for praise.
Some service rendered, some solace given,
And gentle peace with God and heaven.
May your love for one another come second only to your love
for the Lord.

Never be afraid to trust an unknown future to a known God.

Children

Take care with these – don't use them unless the couple are known to be keen to start a family and have no known problems in that area. Don't use them for older couples who already have children from former relationships.

May there be a generation of children
On the children of your children.
May I see you grey and combing your grandchildren's hair.

May your children be blessed with rich parents!

Irish toasts

A great way to get yourself into the good books at an Irish wedding! Some may be adapted for other cultures and situations. If you fancy using the Gaelic expressions at the end, ask an Irish speaker to confirm pronunciation – it rarely bears much relation to how it looks!

Health and a long life to you.
Land without rent to you.
A child every year to you.
And if you can't go to heaven,
May you at least die in Ireland.

May your neighbours respect you,
Trouble neglect you,
The angels protect you,
And heaven accept you.

May your blessings outnumber the shamrocks that grow,
And may trouble avoid you wherever you go.

May the Irish hills caress you.
May her lakes and rivers bless you.
May the luck of the Irish possess you.

May your thoughts be as glad as the shamrocks.
May your hearts be as light as a song.
May each day bring you bright happy hours,
That stay with you all year long.

For each petal on the shamrock
This brings a wish your way
Good health, good luck, and happiness
For today and every day.

May your heart be warm and happy
With the lilt of Irish laughter
Every day in every way
And forever and ever after.

Wherever you go and whatever you do,
May the luck of the Irish be there with you.

May the luck of the Irish enfold you.
May the blessings of Saint Patrick behold you.

May you have warm words on a cold evening,
A full moon on a dark night,
And the road downhill all the way to your door.

May you ...
Work like you don't need the money,
Love like you've never been hurt,
Dance like no one is watching,
Live each day as though it were your last,
And drink like a true Irishman.

Go maire sibh bhur saol nua. ('May you enjoy your new life.')

Sliocht sleacht ar shlioch bhur sleachta. ('Blessings on your posterity.')

Fad saol agat. ('Long life to you.')

Go n-eiri an t-adh leat. ('Good luck.')

Risqué toasts
Only use these if you are sure the audience will appreciate the funny side rather than finding them smutty.

May all your ups and downs come only in the bedroom.

May your wedding night be like a kitchen table – all legs and no drawers.

Here's to wives and girlfriends.
May they never meet!

To women and horses – and the men that ride them!

Tongue-twisters
These ones you'll definitely need to practise if you're likely to have a few drinks beforehand!

Here's a health to all those that we love,
Here's a health to all those that love us,
Here's a health to all those that love them
that love those
that love them
that love those
that love us.

Congratulations on the termination of your isolation and may I express an appreciation of your determination to end the desperation and frustration which has caused you so much consternation in giving you the inspiration to make a combination to bring an accumulation to the population.

Toasts from husband to wife or vice versa
Here's to me and here's to you,
And here's to love and laughter.
I'll be true as long as you
But not a single second after!

To the two secrets to a long-lasting happy marriage:
A good sense of humour – and a short memory!

May we never forget what is worth remembering
Or remember what is best forgotten.

Because I love you truly,
Because you love me, too,
My very greatest happiness
Is sharing life with you.

Here's to you and here's to me,
I hope we never disagree,
But if, perchance, we ever do,
Then here's to me, to hell with you.

Long life and happiness – for your life will be my happiness

A thing of beauty is a joy forever.
Here's to you, my beautiful bride. (John Keats)

To my wife, my bride and joy.
Here's to the woman that's good and sweet,
Here's to the woman that's true,
Here's to the woman that rules my heart,
In other words, here's to you.

Every day you look lovelier and today you look like tomorrow.

Here's to the prettiest, here's to the wittiest,
Here's to the truest of all who are true,
Here's to the neatest one, here's to the sweetest one,
Here's to them, all in one – here's to you.

To my bride: she knows all about me and loves me just the same.

Happy marriages begin when we marry the one we love,
And they blossom when we love the one we married.

Toasts to the bride
Although usually made by the groom (see earlier), another speaker may also make a toast to the bride. These are suitable in this instance; some of those just given could also be adapted.

To the bride – may she share everything with her husband, including the housework.

Here's to the bride. May your hours of joy be as numerous as the petals of your bouquet.

To the bride. Remember we are giving you this husband on approval. He may be returned for credit or exchange, but your love will not be refunded.

Toasts to the groom

The best man often includes a brief, amusing toast to the groom.

To the man who has conquered the bride's heart, and her mother's.

Here's to the groom, a man who keeps his head though he loses his heart.

To the groom: He is leaving us for a better life. But we are not leaving him.

Toasts to friends/guests

A toast to friends or the guests in general is often made by bride or groom.

To the lamp of friendship – may it burn brightest in the darkest hours and never flicker in the winds of trial.

To our best friends – who know the worst about us, but refuse to believe it.

To our guests: May Fortune be as generous with you as she has been in giving us such friends.

Quotations

Below you will find some quotations that you might like to weave into your speech. Only ever use one or two, and only if they are apt and flow well into the rest of the speech. Generally it is best not to *start* a speech with a quote – it's a bit hackneyed – but if you must, at least make it a funny one to get the audience on your side. Many of those shown below are rather tongue-in-cheek, so read carefully and quote with appropriate tone and expression.

In the following, the person quoted is shown in parentheses like this: (Boswell). Notes in square brackets like these [marriage] are not part of the quote.

Always remember to introduce the quote with the name of the person who said or wrote it. If the quote is anonymous (Anon), lead into it with 'As someone once said …'.

About marriage

Marriage is a sort of friendship recognised by the police. (Anon)

They are not said to be husband and wife, who merely sit together. Rather they alone are called husband and wife who have one soul in two bodies. (A Sikh prayer)

Marriage is based on the theory that when a man discovers a particular brand of beer exactly to his taste, he should at once throw in his job and go to work in the brewery. (George Nathan)

Every man should marry – and no woman. (Benjamin Disraeli)

[Marriage is] *the union of hands and hearts.* (Bishop Jeremy Taylor)

Therefore shall a man leave his father and mother, and cleave unto his wife: and they shall be one flesh. (The Bible)

Marriage is a wonderful institution, but who wants to live in an institution? (Groucho Marx)

Strange to say what delight we married people have, to see these poor fools decoyed into our condition. (Samuel Pepys)

In married life three is company and two is none. (Oscar Wilde)

Marriage has many pains, but celibacy has no pleasures.
(Samuel Johnson)

Marriage is popular because it combines the maximum of temptation with the maximum of opportunity.
(George Bernard Shaw)

By all means marry. If you get a good wife you will become happy – if you get a bad one you will become a philosopher.
(Socrates)

Let me not to the marriage of true minds
Admit impediments. Love is not love
Which alters when it alteration finds,
Or tends with the remover to remove:
O no! It is an ever-fixed mark.
(Shakespeare)

It is a woman's business to get married as soon as possible, and
a man's to keep unmarried as long as he can.
(George Bernard Shaw)

I am not against hasty marriages, where a mutual flame is
fanned by an adequate income. (Wilkie Collins)

It doesn't much signify whom one marries, for one is sure to find
next morning that it was someone else. (Samuel Rogers)

Marriage itself is nothing but a civil contract. (John Selden)

The reason why so few marriages are happy is because young
ladies spend their time in making nets [to catch a husband] *not*
in making cages [to keep them]. (Jonathan Swift)

Many a good hanging prevents a bad marriage. (Shakespeare)

Marriage is like life in this – that it is a field of battle and not a bed of roses. (Robert Louis Stevenson)

I was ever of the opinion, that the honest man who married and brought up a large family did more service than he who continued single and only talked of population. (Oliver Goldsmith)

When I said I would die a bachelor, I did not think I should live 'til I were married. (Shakespeare)

There was an old man of Lyme,
Who married three wives at one time.
When asked 'Why the third?'
He replied 'One's absurd...
And bigamy, sir, is a crime.' (Anon)

I would be married but I'd have no wife.
I would be married to a single life. (Richard Crashaw)

About love
Drink to me only with thine eyes,
And I will pledge with mine;
Or leave a kiss within the cup,
And I'll not look for wine. (Ben Jonson)

Love's the noblest frailty of the mind. (John Dryden)

To fall in love is to create a religion that has a fallible god.
(Jorge Luis Borges)

Life has taught us that love does not consist in gazing at each other but in looking outward together in the same direction.
(Antoine de Saint-Exupery)

The best and most beautiful things in the world cannot be seen or even touched. They must be felt with the heart. (Helen Keller)

Love and scandal are the best sweeteners of tea.
(Henry Fielding)

The minute I heard my first love story I started looking for you, not knowing how blind that was. Lovers don't finally meet somewhere. They're in each other all along. (Anon)

This heart of thine, let it be mine.
And this heart of mine, let it be thine. (Anon)

At the touch of love everyone becomes a poet. (Plato)

One word frees us of all the weight and pain in life. That word is love. (Sophocles)

Love is the child of illusion and the parent of disillusion.
(Miguel de Unamuno)

The course of true love never did run smooth. (Shakespeare)

It is impossible to love and to be wise. (George Herbert)

There are truly only four questions that matter:
What is sacred,
Of what is the spirit made,
What is worth living for,
And what is worth dying for?
The answer to all of these is love. It is love, not reason, that is
stronger than death. (Thomas Mann)

The moment is short, but love lasts an eternity – Let it take wing
and fly through your hearts. (Anon)

The man or woman you really love will never grow old to you.
Through the wrinkles of time, through the bowed frame of years,
you will always see the dear face and feel the warm heart union
of your eternal love. (Alfred A. Montapert)

About men, bridegrooms and husbands

Most of these are not particularly complimentary! As such they
work best when used by a woman in a humorous speech.
Choose your words carefully.

Can you imagine a world without men? No crime and lots of happy, fat women. (Marion Smith)

Give a man a free hand and he'll run it all over you. (Mae West)

I never married because I have three pets at home that answer the same purpose as a husband. I have a dog that growls every morning, a parrot that swears all afternoon and a cat that comes home late at night. (Marie Corelli)

Marrying a man is like buying something you've been admiring for a long time in a shop window. You may love it when you get home, but it doesn't always go with everything else in the house. (Jean Kerr)

Before marriage a man will lay awake all night thinking about something you said; after marriage he'll fall asleep before you have finished saying it. (Helen Rowland)

It's not the men in my life that count, it's the life in my men. (Mae West)

An archaeologist is the best husband a woman can have. The older she gets, the more interested he is in her. (Agatha Christie)

I require only three things of a man. He must be handsome, ruthless and stupid. (Dorothy Parker)
A husband is what is left of the lover after the nerve is extracted. (Helen Rowland)

All husbands are alike, but they have different faces so you can tell them apart. (Ogden Nash)

In marriage, a man becomes slack and selfish, and undergoes a fatty degeneration of his moral being. (Robert Louis Stevenson)

The most dangerous food a man can eat is wedding cake. (Anon)

The man who says his wife can't take a joke, forgets that she took him. (Oscar Wilde)

A diplomat is a man who always remembers a woman's birthday but never her age. (Anon)

It's a funny thing that when a man hasn't anything on earth to worry about, he goes off and gets married. (Robert Frost)

A little in drink, but at all times your faithful husband. (Sir Richard Steele)

Being a husband is a whole-time job. (Arnold Bennett)

No worse a husband than the best of men. (Shakespeare)

All women become like their mothers. That is their tragedy. No man does. That is his. (Oscar Wilde)

If the heart of a man is depressed with cares
The mist is dispelled when a woman appears. (John Gay)

He is dreadfully married. He's the most married man I ever saw. (Charles Farrar Brown)

About women, brides and wives

And most (but not all) of these are equally uncomplimentary about the ladies! So use them sparingly and always with humour.

Wives are young men's mistresses
Companions for middle age
And old men's nurses. (Francis Bacon)

Some respite to husbands the weather may send.
But housewives' affairs have never an end. (Thomas Tusser)

If men knew how women pass the time when they are alone, they'd never marry. (W. S. Porter)

Nothing makes a good wife like a good husband. (Anon)

Whoso findeth a wife, findeth a good thing. (The Bible)

Though women are angels, wedlock's the devil. (Byron)

Apologise to a man when you're wrong, but to a woman even if you're right. (Anon)

Any woman can fool a man if she wants to and if he's in love with her. (Agatha Christie)

No man should have a secret from his wife. She invariably finds it out. (Oscar Wilde)

Woman like silent men, they think they are listening. (Marcel Achard)

The trouble with some women is that they get all excited about nothing, and then marry him. (Cher)

I chose my wife, as she did her wedding gown, not for a fine glossy surface, but such qualities as would wear well. (Oliver Goldsmith)

A fellow almost damned in a fair wife. (Shakespeare)

Courtship to marriage [is] *as a very witty prologue to a dull play.*
(William Congreve)

*Let us be very strange and well-bred. Let us be as strange as if
we had been married a great while; and as well-bred as if we
were not married at all.* (William Congreve)

*It is a truth universally acknowledged, that a single man in
possession of a good fortune, must be in want of a wife.*
(Jane Austen)

*One wife is too much for most husbands to hear
But two at a time there's no mortal can bear.* (John Gay)

*What is it then to have or have no wife
But single thraldom or a double strife?*
(Francis Bacon)

*Boys will be boys. And even that wouldn't matter if we could
only prevent girls from being girls.* (Sir Anthony Hope)

Behind every great man there is a surprised woman.
(Maryon Pearson)

Bridesmaids

There are few of these, but you can always supplement them with plenty of compliments!

A happy bridesmaid makes a happy bride. (Tennyson)

Always the bridesmaid, never the bride. (Anon)

Second marriages

Only use these if it is generally known that this is a second marriage, and where the humour would be appreciated. Otherwise, most of the quotes given would be equally suitable at a second wedding.

When widows exclaim loudly against second marriage, I would always lay wager that the man, if not the wedding day, is absolutely fixed upon. (Henry Fielding)

We are number two. We try harder.
(Avis Car Rental advertisement)

For I'm not so old, and not so plain.
And I'm quite prepared to marry again. (W. S. Gilbert)

Where to Find Out More

Below are some books and web sites that you may find useful as sources of information or inspiration for your speech.

Books

There are hundreds of speechwriting books available, but the following are particularly aimed at the first-time wedding speaker. All are available from good bookshops or the many online retailers such as Amazon or BOL.com

Making a Wedding Speech, John Bowden (How To Books)

Mitch Murray's One-Liners for Weddings, Mitch Murray (Foulsham)

Mitch Murray's Handbook for the Terrified Speaker, Mitch Murray (Foulsham)

Wedding Speeches, Lee Jarvis (Foulsham)

Wedding Speeches and Toasts, Barbara Jeffery (Foulsham)

Quotes on all subjects, including many on marriage and family, can be found in:

The Oxford Dictionary of Quotations (Oxford University Press)

The Penguin Dictionary of Quotations (Penguin)

Guidance on your wider role in the wedding plans overall can be found in:

The Best Best Man, Jacqueline Eames (Foulsham)

The Best Man's Organiser, Christopher Hobson (Foulsham)

Essentials: Wedding Duties for Men, Carole Chapman (Foulsham)

Web sites

The following are general wedding-related sites, usually offering a wide variety of services from gowns to flowers, place-cards to confetti. Each has a section on speeches and toasts, but they vary in length and usefulness.

www.2-in-2-1.com

www.confetti.co.uk

www.hitched.co.uk

www.ourmarriage.com

www.weddingbells.com

www.weddings-and-brides.co.uk

www.weddingchannel.com

www.weddingguide.co.uk

For information on the content of civil ceremonies in the UK, see: www.registerofficeweddings.com

The following are sites dedicated to speeches of various types, or public speaking in general. Most provide guidance on speechwriting and presentation; some will provide a personalised speech for you, if you pay the appropriate fee.

www.occasionalwords.com

www.speech-writers.com

www.speeches.com

www.scripttease.co.uk

www.davegustafson.com/speech

If you intend using a projector or video, check out the presenting tips at

www.presentingsolutions.com/effectivepresentations.html
Although aimed primarily at business speakers, the advice is equally suitable for weddings.

The following sites give useful information (not necessarily speeches) for weddings of different faiths or cultures, or details of traditions in particular countries – useful if you have not attended such a wedding before.

A quick guide to wedding traditions of almost any faith or culture can be found at the Roses USA site. Go to:

www.rosesusa.com/weddings/aborigine.cfm
and use the drop-down list to find the page you require.

The following site also has discussions and personal experiences of a variety of interfaith weddings, including details of traditions and taboos:

www.beliefnet.com

For details of traditional wedding etiquette and customs in a particular country, try:

www.ourmarriage.com/html/around_the_world.html

For specific faiths/cultures, see also the following sites, which give more detail:

Hindi:
www.lalwani.demon.co.uk/sonney/wedding.htm
www.mybindi.com/weddings/ceremonies/hindu.cfm

Humanist:
www.suffolkhumanists.org.uk/ceremonies/index.htm#WEDDINGS
www.humanism.org.uk/weddings

Jewish:
www.jewish.org.pl/english/edu/JewFAQ/marriage.htm
www.beingjewish.com/cycle/wedding.html

Mormon:
www.ldsweddings.com/sacred/sacred1.html

www.templemarriage.com

Muslim:
matrimonial.allindiamart.com/muslim.htm

www.mybindi.com/weddings/ceremonies/muslim.cfm

Sikh:
www.sikhs.org/wedding

www.mybindi.com/weddings/ceremonies/sikh.cfm

matrimonial.allindiamart.com/sikh.htm

Index